MW00638443

Mountain Biking Mammoth

Mountain Bike Trails of Mammoth Mountain, Bishop, June Lake, & Beyond

Dave & Allison Diller

E(X)TREMELINE
PRODUCTIONS LLC

2005

www.EXTREMELINE.com

Please Read This Important Information Before Using This Book!

Table of Contents

Special Thanks

Thanks to our friends and everyone who helped us create this book! Big shouts of gratitude go out to those at Mammoth Mountain Bike Park; Dave Geirman, Alex Fabbro, and Julie Brown.

We appreciate the help from the Inyo National Forest and Sandy Hogan. Thanks to Nate Greenberg for your cooperation with GIS information, and to Cindy Whitehead Buccowich for stopping for the photo!   We are also grateful for Andrew Pernicano's keen artistic eye and help with the cover!

And of course we are so thankful to friends and family who helped with rides, pictures and inspiration: Dave and Nicole Brooks, Jay and Kira Brown, Dave Thompson, Jeff and Leanna Block, Andrew and Martina Pernicano and Charlie, Jeff Behl, Shelly, Scott Shear, Mark and Susanna Neave, John and Margie Block, and Jon Moynier.

Mountain bike legend, Cindy Whitehead Buccowich,
on a morning ride above Red's Lake.

Mammoth Rides Map

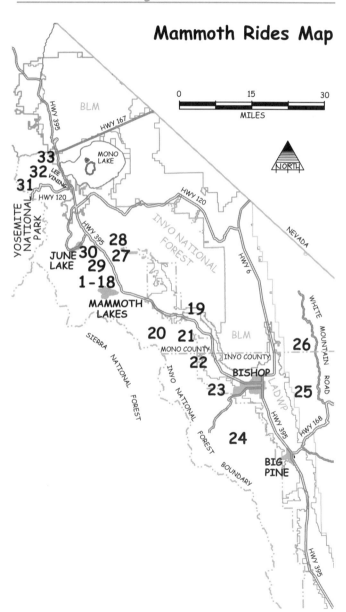

Welcome To Mammoth

Encompassed by public lands, Mammoth offers one of the most varied and beautiful environments on the planet. This West Coast mecca of mountain biking is ideally situated at the juncture of the gorgeous Eastern Sierra slope and the surreal Great Basin high desert. With wonderful weather and a stupendous landscape filled with trails, Mammoth defines the

Excersize is just the side effect up here!

meaning of outdoor paradise. Mountain biking here will not only thrill you, it will make you stoked on life! You will find yourself completely immersed in nature; whether riding around a pristine alpine lake that reflects ancient glaciered peaks, or flying down singletrack through a volcanic wonderland, or weaving along clear trout-filled creeks in pine and fir forests. Furthermore, abundant wildlife and 1800's historical relics will often add an exhilarating surprise to anyone's ride!

There are plenty of options for all ability levels whether you want a scenic family ride or a gnarly downhill technical challenge. Caution; mountain biking here can be extremely addictive!

About This Guidebook

Another day of play in Mammoth Mountain Bike Park.

The Book

This pocket-sized guide is meant to be as trans-portable and versatile as a mountain biker. While providing specific information about mountain biking in Mammoth, it will aid you in choosing and locating appropriate trails and rides.

This book is categorized into four sections based on location: Mammoth Mountain, Mammoth Area Trails, South of Mammoth, and North of Mammoth. Trail details and directions are provided for each ride along with accurate maps and elevation profiles, created with the latest GPS mapping technology. These elements will help enable you, the biker, to have the freedom and ability to piece together your own perfect biking adventure.

Ratings and Ride Details

Location: General area of the ride.

Distance: Measured in miles, based on a calibrated odometer. Take into consideration that individual bike computers may be calibrated differently and depict varying mileages.

Elevation: Depicts the minimum and maximum elevation you will encounter on the ride.

Trail Surface: Explains what kind of trail you'll be riding.

Singletrack is a narrow trail ideal for mountain biking.

Mx Trail is a trail that is often used by motorcycles and is a little wider than singletrack, often having "whoops" and banked turns. Unfortunately, 4-wheel all-terrain vehicles (ATV) often follow the motorcycle tracks, creating ever-widening trails.

<u>Dirt Road</u> is what it sounds like; usually a further explanation will describe if it is narrow, wide, graded, or doubletrack.

Type of Ride: Defines the ride as a Loop, Out & Back, or One-Way.

Terrain: Tells you about the surrounding environment and scenery of the ride.

Technical Level: Describes how difficult the trail is to bike, relative to other Mammoth area trails.

<u>Easy:</u> Usually a mostly smooth and wide trail or dirt road.

<u>Medium:</u> Some tree roots, ruts, rocks, and/or potholes with some maneuvering involved; usually on a tighter trail.

<u>Difficult:</u> Narrow trail with bigger tree roots, ruts, drop-offs, and/or rocks; steep sections.

<u>Most Difficult:</u> Steep and rough, large obstacles, frequent changes in gradient; hike-n-bike likely in some sections.

Exertion Level: The general aerobic level of a ride.

<u>Mild</u>: For the most part, the ride is flat with little or no climbing.

<u>Moderate</u>: Hills with some gradual or short steep climbs.

<u>Strenuous</u>: Longer & steeper uphill sections that may cause excessive panting and sweating.

<u>Very Strenuous</u>: Heart pounding, mega uphill sections.

Highlights: A brief description of the main features of the ride to get you pumped up!

Options: Ways to lengthen, shorten, or add variety to the ride.

Note: Anything deserving attention about the ride.

Directions/Access: Specific directions to the trailhead. Sometimes directions refer to "North Village," which is at the junction of Lake Mary Road, HWY 203, and Minaret Road.

Ride Profile: This graph depicts the ride in terms of elevation gain and loss related to mileage - so you know what to expect. The major changes in elevation and key features are shown. Please keep in mind that the scope of the profiles may require that quick changes in elevation be left out. Because of the variety in the elevation and length of different rides depicted, exact comparisons between profiles can not be made without taking these factors into account.

Mileage Guide: Provides key features and a description of the ride to help prevent you from getting lost. These are labeled in miles for those with either bike computers or mathematically gifted minds. Mileages may vary among individual bike computers.

Map Legend

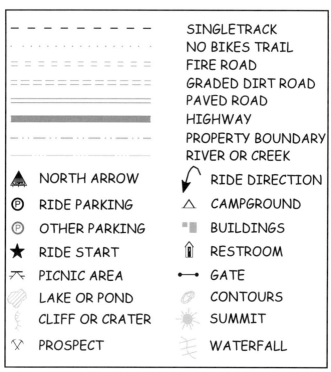

– – – – – – – – –	SINGLETRACK
· · · · · · · · ·	NO BIKES TRAIL
= = = = = = = =	FIRE ROAD
= = = = = = = =	GRADED DIRT ROAD
	PAVED ROAD
	HIGHWAY
· — · — · — · — ·	PROPERTY BOUNDARY
	RIVER OR CREEK
▲ NORTH ARROW	↵ RIDE DIRECTION
℗ RIDE PARKING	△ CAMPGROUND
℗ OTHER PARKING	▪▐ BUILDINGS
★ RIDE START	⌂ RESTROOM
⋻ PICNIC AREA	•—• GATE
▱ LAKE OR POND	◌ CONTOURS
⌇ CLIFF OR CRATER	☀ SUMMIT
⋎ PROSPECT	≋ WATERFALL

Index of Top 3 Rides by Category Use this short index as a basic reference tool to select what kind of ride you prefer; whether it be Sweet Singletrack, Cross Country Rides, Easy Cruisers, Quick Fixes, Insane Downhills, Expedition Rides, Hardcore Climbs, or Mammoth Classics. See Page 203.

About Mammoth

Mammoth's Past

Situated on the edge of the Long Valley Caldera, an ancient but active volcanic region, lies Mammoth Mountain. While nearby eruptions have happened as recently as the 18th century, this composite volcano formed almost 200,000 years ago and has exploded as recently as 50,000 years ago. The landscape is filled with testimony to this catastrophic history. Cinder cones, craters, obsidian domes, Hot Creek, and pyroclastic flows are all witness to its violent past.

Ancient volcanic rock provides the ultimate challenge for the NORBA Downhill National Championships.

As time pressed on, the fiery ordeals shared history with intermittent glacial periods. Just as hot magma formed the land, ice shaped the rugged Sierras. Glaciers slowly carved out valleys and cragged peaks, leaving the majestic scenery you see today.

By 500 A.D., the lake and forest-filled ecosystem had inevitably attracted the Native Americans. The Mono Lake Paiutes settled and traded the region's natural resources, such as obsidian used for making arrowheads and tools.

Before long the Gold Rush of the middle to late 1800's brought gold-prospecting folks into Paiute lands. By the 1880's the area between Mineral Hill of the Sherwin Range and Mammoth "Pumice" Mountain was transformed into a wild west mining town. Named after the well marketed mining claim, Mammoth Mine, the town hustled and bustled for a few short years. But as the harsh realities of gold mining in the Eastern Sierra set in, "Mammoth City" went the way of the ghost town.

It wasn't too long, however, before a new generation of adventurers and tourists started checking out the area. In the 1930's, Dave McCoy was toying around with small rope tows for skiing. Finding the ideal location, he settled on Mammoth Mountain in the 1940's and downhill skiers have accumulated on the mountain ever since.

To share in the fun, mountain bikers blew on the scene in 1985 with the famed race, Kamikaze. At Mammoth Mountain, Bill Cockroft was instrumental in creating and promoting downhill races and the first NORBA World Championships in the late 1980's. At this time, one of the first official mountain bike parks in the world was developed on the ski slopes of Mammoth. The races here have had some of the largest attended mountain biking events in the U.S. Since this time, Mammoth Mountain has been expanding and improving the park, and biking has spread into the entire region.

Chasing shadows in the Eastern Sierra sun.

Getting Around

Travelling to Mammoth Lakes

Most people hop in the car and drive. If you happen to have access to a private plane, Mammoth has its own airport to accommodate you, 760.934.8989. Otherwise, the closest commercial airports are in Los Angeles or Reno. Bus transportation is available via "The C.R.E.S.T." which runs along HWY 395 from the Reno Airport to Ridgecrest. Call The Crest for details; 760.872.1901.

Travelling in Mammoth Lakes

Once in Mammoth, cars are not necessary, since the Town is developing quality summer bus transportation for visitors. More importantly, Mammoth is biker-friendly and numerous bike paths make it easy to get around (see p. 120)!

Summer driving distances from various cities:

Los Angeles: 344 miles.   **San Francisco:** 260 miles.
San Diego: 404 miles.   **Las Vegas:** 307 miles.
Santa Barbara: 367 miles   **Reno:** 167 miles.
South Lake Tahoe: 140 miles.

High Country Climate and Weather

The weather in the Eastern Sierra can be as extreme as the local mountain bikers. While summers are usually perfectly sunny and in the high 70 degree range, thunderstorms and high winds can bring some variety to the day. Late spring and early fall may easily bring surprise snow showers. The weather for riding is usually ideal between late June and early October for the higher elevations, such as on Mammoth Mountain. The weather often cooperates for riding as early as March/April and as late as November/December for many of the lower elevation trails, such as at Lower Rock Creek Trail and Deep Canyon Trail in the Tungsten Hills.

Sun

In the Eastern Sierra the sun is strong and almost always shining. There's far less UV-filtering atmosphere between the sun and Mammoth, than when you are at the beach. So the point is: wear your sunscreen!

Elevation

The elevation in this part of the Sierras is very high and ranges quite a bit. When riding on Mammoth Mountain, it is possible to ride from 11,000 feet down to 7,000 feet in a relatively short amount of time. At these high elevations, the body requires more water, so bring plenty. Some people need to adjust to the altitude before hardcore aerobic exercise. A windbreaker is also a very good idea, especially at the top of Mammoth Mountain, where it is often windy. As a general rule, the temperature decreases 5.5 degrees for every 1,000 foot gain in elevation. Not including wind chill, the top of Mammoth Mountain can be at least 22 degrees cooler than the town of Mammoth Lakes.

Average High and Low Temperatures (F)

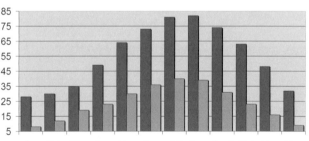

Monthly Sunrise Times (AM Standard Time)**

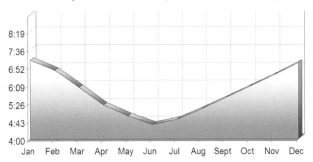

Monthly Sunset Times (PM Standard Time)**

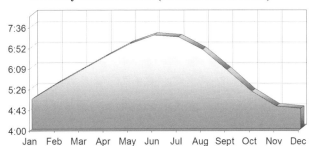

** Times on charts above are depicted in Standard Time. Add 1 hour for Day Light Savings Time (DST).

Other Considerations

Bears
There are a lot of Black Bears in and around the Mammoth area. You are much more likely to see one rummaging through a dumpster than one out on the trail. However, you may very well see bear scat on the trail. If you do see one on the trail, avoid confrontation and do not approach it. Stay away especially if you see cubs; mothers are dangerous! While in town, don't leave food in your cars and be cautious around trash bins at night!

Multi-Use Trails

Many of the trails around Mammoth are "multi-use", meaning that horses, hikers, and/or motorcycles may appear at anytime. Please be cautious and alert when riding. Always be considerate to all the users. Many good trails have been closed due to conflict between horses and bikers. Lets change that. Bikers must yield to both hikers and horse riders.

Pumice

This is the white-gray stuff that is all over Mammoth. Pumice is a very light, porous igneous rock that was created during Mammoth's past volcanic eruptions. It formed when liquid silica was violently expelled from cinder cones and gas bubbles were trapped as it cooled and solidified. Not only does this make it extremely light, it makes for a very rough texture with many cavities.

Bikers new to the Mammoth area may find riding a bit different with the looser soil. If you charge hard, you may find yourself flying over the handlebars at first. Pumice is rough on the skin, but soft on the bones. After being bucked off the bike, most will learn a quick trick: Keep your weight over the back wheel! Hanging your butt off the back of the seat will help on steep descents. Also, avoid using the front brakes in corners and turn the handlebars as little as possible. Sharp turns will dig the front tire into deep pumice. Instead, try to turn more by leaning your body weight. Big tires also help quite a bit. When going uphill, get in the lowest gear and bomb up!

Wilderness

"Wilderness" is a government-designated category of land-use aimed to preserve the land in its natural state. No "mechanized" forms of travel, such as bicycles, are allowed. Hiking and horseback riding are the only permissible forms of travel. So if you are on a bike, STAY out of Wilderness! Riding in these areas is very illegal (with huge fines for trail poachers) and devastates the overall mountain biking cause.

IMBA'S Trail Rules

Across the country thousands of miles of dirt trails have been closed to mountain bicyclists in recent years. The irresponsible riding habits of a few riders have been a factor. Do your part to maintain trail access by observing the following rules of the trail, formulated by IMBA (International Mountain Bicycling Association). Extensive mountain bike and trail access information can be found on their website: www.imba.com.

1. Ride on open trails only.
2. Leave no trace.
3. Control your bicycle.
4. Always yield trail.
5. Never spook animals.
6. Plan ahead.

Author's Trail Law

Respect all of creation for your enjoyment and for all those who follow. Use common sense and keep mountain bike trails open by respecting the rules. Always be joyful, ride your best, and have lots of fun!

Singletrack

If you would like to see more singletrack opened to the public, become involved politically by contacting elected officials and joining a mountain bike advocacy group such as Mammoth Area Mountain Bike Association (MAMBA). As more mountain bikers voice their opinions, politicians and land managers will be forced to listen. As the authors would absolutely love to see more singletrack open to bikers, this book strongly encourages bikers to respect the laws and ride the many designated trails.

Mammoth Mountain Bike Park

Disneyland at 9000 feet.

How does 80 miles of sweet singletrack on a 3,500 acre mountain with over 3,000 feet of vertical drop sound? What about continuous banked s-turns that rhythmically slalom through a High Sierra strand of white barked pine? Or, an awe-inspiring cross-country loop that winds its way in and out of forests, around a lake, leading to Backpacker Magazine covershot-type views of the jagged Minarets and dramatic Yosemite area peaks? Awake yet?! How about bombing gnarly rock chutes and hitting massive jumps and drops on any of the raging downhiller/freeride trails

Isn't this cheating?

in the Park! Welcome to the world famous Mammoth Mountain Bike Park!

The Bike Park has kept in line with the legacy it started with the Kamikaze race in the 1980's. With jaw-dropping scenery and trails for all ages and ability levels, the Bike Park has become an

Thundershowers make the trails goooooood!

epicenter for West Coast mountain biking. It is no wonder that the premier professional bike race, the NORBA National Finals, is held at Mammoth Mountain!

Basics

The Mammoth Mountain Bike Park headquarters is located at the Adventure Center near Main Lodge, and is usually open from late June through September. The trails are open from 9:30am to 5:30pm daily in the summer. Updated information on prices and trail conditions can be found on the website, *www.mammothmountain.com,* or by calling 1.800.MAM-MOTH. Pedal passes are available, as well as full passes that include use of the Panorama Gondola and the Bike Shuttle. The Bike Shuttle runs every 20 minutes and waits near the Village Gondola on Canyon Blvd.

Safety

The trails are patrolled by rangers who are available to help bikers and enforce the rules. While every rider should be as self-sufficient as possible, bike park rangers can help with fixing flats, injuries, and other problems. Due to the nature of the trails on the mountain, proper safety equipment is a must! Although it may be overkill for some bikers, full-face helmets

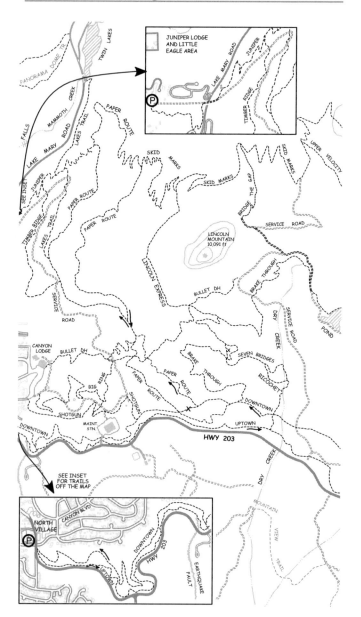

MAMMOTH MOUNTAIN BIKE PARK

and body armor (elbow and knee pads, shin guards, etc.) are quickly gaining popularity in this part of the biking world. Water and maps are offered in tented rest areas scattered about the park. These are currently located at the intersection of Paper Route and Big Ring, and at the Uptown and Downtown trails near the maintenance garage. Restrooms and emergency phones are available at North Village, McCoy Station, Mammoth Adventure Center, Panorama Lookout/Upper Gondola, and at the Outpost near Reds Lake.

X-Zones

One of the coolest features of the Bike Park are the X-Zones. They are steeper and more advanced sections of trail that cut off a switchback of a main trail. Catering to the new freerider and downhiller-type of biker, the X-Zones each have their own unique jumps, drops, and technical sections. There are X-Zones off of Paper Route, Beach Cruiser, Bearing Straits, Brake Through, Kamikaze, and Chain Smoke. New freeride areas in 2005 are the Twilight Zone and the Kamikaze Park!

Landing gear extended in the X-Zone.

NORBA Racing

In 2004, the NORBA US Mountain Bike National Championship returned to its historic site at Mammoth Mountain after a brief respite for a couple years. This premier mounting biking event crowns the national and category champions, and exhibits the original mountain bike race: The Kamikaze Downhill! Categories featured at the US Nationals are Cross-Country, Short Track, Super D, Downhill, Mountain

Cross-country racers competing in the NORBA
National Championships.

Cross, Observed Trials, Single Speed, and Marathon. Adding to the excitement is an outdoor bike festival with entertainment and family events. This event occurs in late September; call 1.800.MAMMOTH for updates.

Off The Top

Location: Drops from the summit down the backside.
Distance: 5.5 miles to Beach Cruiser.
  4.4 miles to Gravy Train and Kamikaze turnoff.
Elevation: 11020/9300 ft.
Trail Surface: 100% singletrack.
Type of Ride: Ridden downhill; although some ride up from the Beach Cruiser Loop, it's not advisable during park hours.
Terrain: Pumice; sparse forest; vast western Sierra views.
Technical Level: Medium.
Exertion Level: Mild; some pedaling with a lot of coasting.

*The grandiose surroundings are noted by the relative
size of the rider in the foreground.*

Highlights: The most popular of the upper trails, Off the Top
starts on the desolate backside slope of Mammoth Mountain,
with unsurpassed views of the Sierras and San Joaquin River
valley to the west. After a series of switchbacks, the trail leads
below the timberline, becoming more curvy with an occasional tree root obstacle. Off The Top leads to Beach Cruiser,
Kamikaze, or Gravy Train.

Beach Cruiser

An ascent of Beach Cruiser on a summer day may tempt some into the cool clear waters of Reds Lake.

Location: Northwest side of the mountain.

Distance: 6.1-mile loop.

From Off The Top to Mountain View turnoff : 1 mile.

From Off The Top to Adventure Center: 3.2 miles.

From Off The Top to X-Zone: 2.2 miles.

From trailhead up to Bearing Straits/Kamikaze: 2.5 miles.

From trailhead up to Off The Top turnoff: 2.9 miles.

Elevation: 9400/8900 ft.

Trail Surface: Mostly singletrack; short sections of service road.

Type of Ride: Directional loop, or descent from Off the Top.

Terrain: Small lake; pumice beach; pine forest; open views.

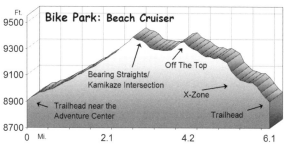

Technical Level: Medium; a few fun-sized tree root dropoffs.
Exertion Level: Moderate; gradual climbing on the full loop, and a short climb when riding downhill from Off The Top.

Highlights: With serene views of Reds Lake, the Minaret Range, and San Joaquin Ridge, Beach Cruiser is undoubtedly

a favorite among bike park riders. This winding roller coaster-type trail will elate most riders. Moreover, the trail has a remote backcountry feeling, especially when riding the full loop. For extra thrills, don't miss the X-Zone!

Dropping in to Beach Cruiser's X-Zone!

Mountain View

Location: Off Beach Cruiser above Reds Lake.
Distance: 1 mile. (A USFS trail continues another ¼ miles to HWY 203, which leads to Minaret Summit and on to the USFS designated Mountain View Trail; Ride 3).
Elevation: 9300/9180 ft.
Trail Surface: 100% singletrack.
Type of Ride: An alternative section off Beach Cruiser.
Terrain: Mountain ridge; striking overlooks; forest.
Technical Level: Medium.

The aptly-named Mountain View Trail.

Exertion Level: Moderate.

Highlights: Given its proximity, this trail has a similar feel to Beach Cruiser. However, it is filled with stupendous views of the Minarets and San Joaquin Ridge, and even looks down the San Joaquin Valley! If you are in need of a natural high, this trail is your drug.

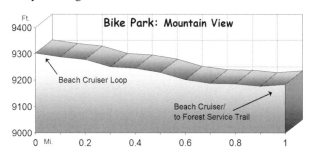

Kamikaze

*With the speed you'll gain on this descent, there will
be little time to enjoy that colossal skyline!*

Location: Descends from the top of the mountain to Main Lodge.
Distance: 3.4 miles.
  Top Trailhead to Gravy Train turnoff: 1.9 miles.
  Top to Beach Cruiser/Bearing Straits/X Zone: 2.3 miles.
  Top Trailhead to lower X-Zone: 3.2 miles.
Elevation: 11,000/8910 ft.
Trail Surface: 100% dirt road.
Type of Ride: Fast downhill road; although spandex-toting
hammerheads are occasionally seen pedaling up it.

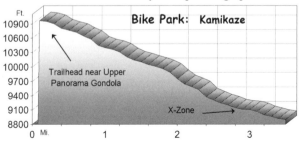

Terrain: Mount Ritter & Banner; Reds Lake; San Joaquin Ridge; mountain slope; pumice.

Technical Level: Medium; steep rough road with loose soil.

Exertion Level: Mild; but tough on the braking muscles.

Highlights: Feeling the need for speed? Kamikaze, a rippin' fast dirt road with bumps, is a 2100-foot drop in less than five minutes! This is the route of the original Kamikaze Downhill, one of the first races that helped bring mountain biking into the realm of cool sports. Letting go of the brakes, puts you above 30 mph in just a few seconds. An X-Zone waits at the bottom!

Upper Velocity

Entering a near-vertical chute on Upper Velocity.

Location: Drops from Skid Marks to Velocity by McCoy Station.

Distance: 1.3 miles.

Elevation: 10,400/9600 ft.

Trail Surface: Mostly singletrack.

Type of Ride: One-Way downhill trail.

Terrain: Boulders; deep pumice; rock chutes; steep slopes.
Technical Level: Most Difficult; very steep, loose soil, very technical boulder sections.
Exertion Level: Moderate; it takes some energy to get through the initial deep pumice section.

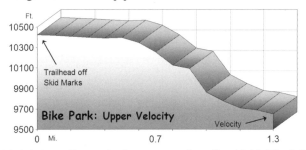

Highlights: Get ready for a mega adrenaline kick! The initial portion of the trail is lame; flat with deep pumice. However, before you know it, the circumstances of life change. The distant eastern mountain ranges pass from sight unnoticed as you clutch the brakes and hang on for dear life! The site of NORBA national downhill races, this is a full-face helmet and body armor type-of-ride.

Velocity

Location: Descends from McCoy Station to the Adventure Center.
Distance: .8 miles.
Elevation: 9600/8910 ft.
Trail Surface: 100% singletrack with rocks, jumps, gaps, logs.
Type of Ride: One-way downhiller/freeride trail.
Terrain: Forest; ski runs; manmade hits and natural drops.
Technical Level: Most Difficult; steep with big obstacles.
Exertion Level: Mild/Moderate.
Highlights: As the continuation of Upper Velocity, this trail is

Com'on, air it you chicken!

fast technical riding for the gnarly crew! Accessed by the mid-station gondola, the trail starts near McCoy station and flies down to Main Lodge near the Adventure Center. A championship downhill course with a humongous gap-jump, speedy straight-aways, steep chutes, jibs, pumice, ledges, jumps, gaps, rocks, ruts, logs ....need we say more?

A bigger-than-it-looks log drop on Velocity.

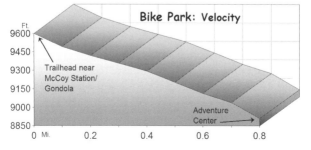

Bike Park: Velocity

Trailhead near McCoy Station/ Gondola

Adventure Center

Chain Smoke

The quickest way down isn't the easiest!

Location: Drops from McCoy Station to the Adventure Center.
Distance: 1.1 miles.
Elevation: 9600/8910 ft.
Trail Surface: 100% singletrack with varied terrain.
Type of Ride: One-way fast downhiller/freeride trail.
Terrain: Trees; jumps; cliffs; rocks; logs; roots; berms; packed dirt and pumice.
Technical Level: Very Difficult.
Exertion Level: Moderate.

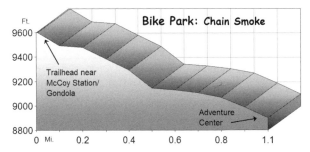

Highlights: To thrill-seekers who thrive on big air and technical challenges: Chain Smoke may enrapture you to cloud nine! This trail rocks! One of the newest trails to be created for the Bike Park, Chain Smoke embodies everything that induces adrenaline in downhill mountain biking: banked turns, doubles, log rides, bendy singletrack, and technical rock sections. Just when you think its over, a large X-Zone awaits at the bottom. One could spend the entire day riding the trail and never get bored. If you're an advanced rider, go out and see for yourself!

Defining the utility of full suspension.

Trail Home

Location: Descends from McCoy Station to the Adventure Center.
Distance: 2.5 miles.
Elevation: 9600/8910 ft.
Trail Surface: 100% singletrack.
Type of Ride: Usually ridden one-way downhill.
Terrain: Open ski run face; sparse forest; summit sightings.
Technical Level: Moderate; bumpy with some tight turns.
Exertion Level: Mild; when riding downhill.

The Trail Home.

Highlights: Trail Home switchbacks its way down the mountainside to the Broadway Express lift. As it is moderately steep with some bumpy maneuvering involved around small rock obstacles, this trail is a great skill-testing run before tackling the tougher trails. Overall, it's a fun ride!

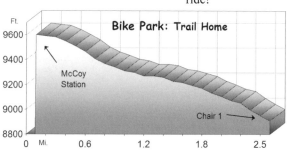

Gravy Train

Location: Traverses the middle of the mountain.

Distance: 1.5 miles

McCoy Station Trailhead to Trail Home turnoff: .1 miles.

McCoy Station Trailhead to Bearing Straits: .8 miles.

McCoy Station Trailhead to Kamikaze: 1.4 miles

McCoy Station Trailhead to Off The Top: 1.5 miles.

Elevation: 9570/9720 ft.

Trail Surface: 100% singletrack.

Type of Ride: Ridden either direction to access various trails.

Terrain: Boulders; some trees; open mountain face; views.

Technical Level: Easy/Medium; some rocks but mostly smooth packed pumice.

Exertion Level: Moderate; mild ups and downs.

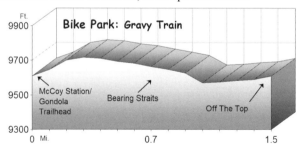

Highlights: Gravy Train is an easily accessible cross-country type of trail. Although it is relatively flat, it requires some pedaling. With a marvelous northeastern outlook, this is a great singletrack addition to vary your riding and connect other trails from either side of the mountain.

Bearing Straits

Location: On the northwest face of Mammoth Mountain.
Distance: 1.8 miles.
Elevation: 9660/9350 ft.
Trail Surface: 100% singletrack.
Type of Ride: Usually ridden downhill from Gravy Train.
Terrain: Boulders; open mountain face; forested areas.
Technical Level: Medium; lots of rocks in the top section.
Exertion Level: Mild/Moderate.

A preview of the mountain biker afterlife.

Highlights: Never too technical or steep, Bearing Straits
swirls its way across a massive open slope and down into the

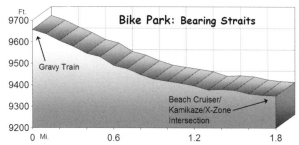

forest. There's just enough rocks, small tree root jumps, and fast straight-aways to make it exciting. It's a great all-around trail for most abilities, ending at an intersection of Beach Cruiser, Kamikaze, and an X-Zone.

Uptown Trail

Location: Ascends from North Village to the Adventure Center.
Distance: 4.7 miles.
  Trailhead to Scenic Loop turnoff: 1 mile.
  Trailhead to Mountain View Trail turnoff: 1.9 miles.
Elevation: 8050/8850 ft.
Trail Surface: 100% singletrack.
Type of Ride: One-way uphill trail.
Terrain: Parallels HWY 203; shady pine and fir forest.

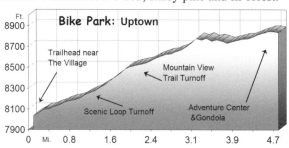

Technical Level: Easy/Medium.
Exertion Level: Moderate/Strenuous.

Highlights: This smoothly-packed singletrack gradually climbs from The Village to the Adventure Center on Mammoth Mountain.

Uptown, a splendid warm-up for the downhill trails, makes a natural loop with Downtown Trail. It can conveniently be merged with other mountain trails for any length of cross country loop. The lower

Spandex are still cool on Uptown.

trail (Ride 1) is open to the public and accesses both Mountain View Trail (Ride 3) and the Scenic Loop Trail (Ride 10).

Downtown Trail

Location: Descends from Mammoth Mountain to the Village.
Distance: 5.4 miles.
  From top near Chain Smoke to Seven Bridges: .8 miles.
  From Seven Bridges to Brake Through: .2 miles.
  From Brake Through to lower Paper Route: .5 miles.
  From Paper Route to Shotgun: .3 miles.
  From Shotgun to Big Ring turnoff: .5 miles.
  From Big Ring turnoff to bottom: 2.9 miles.
Elevation: 8900/8050 ft.
Trail Surface: 100% singletrack.
Type of Ride: One-way descent.
Terrain: Parallels Uptown Trail through shady pine & fir forest.

Rolling down Mammoth's most popular trail.

Technical Level: Medium; mostly easy and relatively smooth, but still some bumps and ruts.

Exertion Level: Mild/Moderate; two short uphill sections.

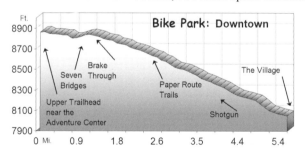

Highlights: Downtown Trail is Mammoth's premiere intermediate/beginner singletrack that advanced bikers love as well! With bermed turns and flowing curves, this is one of the busiest trails in the Park. Many of the other Bike Park trails meld into Downtown at some point, leading riders back down to the bike shuttle. This classic trail is bound to please!

Brake Through

Reveling in the singletrack splendor of Brake Through.

Location: Drops from McCoy Station to Downtown Trail.

Distance: 3.4 miles.

Upper trailhead to Bridge the Gap (and to Bullet): .4 miles.

Upper trailhead to Lincoln Express: 1.6 miles.

Upper trailhead to X-Zone: 2.1 miles.

Upper trailhead to Seven Bridges: 2.3 miles.

Elevation: 9650/8770 ft.

Trail Surface: 100% singletrack.

Type of Ride: Usually one-way downhill/cross-country trail,

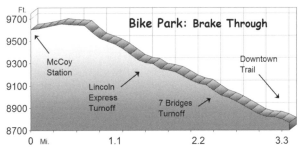

but can be ridden uphill for those with pedal passes.

Terrain: Pine & fir forest; eastern views; packed pumice.

Technical Level: Medium/Difficult; the top is steeper with bumps, rocky segments, a fairly deep pumice section.

Exertion Level: Moderate; some flat and slight uphill segments.

Riding with views of Deer Mountain and prehistoric volcanic features in the background.

Highlights: Brake Through is a superb section of singletrack dropping from McCoy Station to Downtown Trail. The first .2 miles are flat as you cruise around the pond, which are followed by some short ups and downs before it really gets ripping! As the trail snakes down, there are smooth fast sections intermixed with a few rocky, technical challenges. Part way down, the X-Zone adds an optional challenge. The trail definitely becomes more mild and suitable to less experienced riders below the 7 Bridges split off.

Seven Bridges

Location: Descends from Brake Through to Downtown.

Distance: .9 miles.

  Upper trailhead to top of Ricochet: .3 miles.

  Top of Ricochet to lower re-entry of Ricochet: .3 miles.

  Ricochet re-entry to Downtown turnoff: .2 miles.

  Downtown turnoff to end at Uptown: .1 miles.

Watch for trolls lurking near the bridges.

Elevation: 9090/8840 ft.
Trail Surface: 100% singletrack.
Type of Ride: One-way downhill.
Terrain: Forest; Dry Creek; rocky faces; bridges; natural stunts.
Technical Level: Medium/Difficult; rocks and drop-offs.
Exertion Level: Mild.

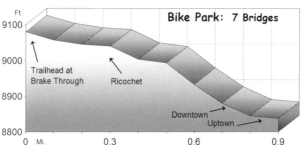

Highlights: 7 Bridges is super twisty with moderate-level natural obstacles and jumps. The trail just seems to get better and better as you ride down; the highlight is zipping back and forth across Dry Creek over the 7 bridges! Go carve this wave of a trail!

Ricochet

Location: A shortcut trail off of Seven Bridges.
Distance: .2 miles.
Elevation: 9040/8950 ft.
Trail Surface: 100% singletrack.
Type of Ride: Downhill section; almost X-Zone-ish.
Terrain: Forest; rocks.
Technical Level: Difficult.
Exertion Level: Mild.

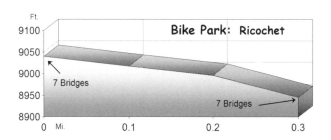

Highlights: The more aggressive riders may want to take this spur off of Seven Bridges. Ricochet consists of technical segments with small log and root jumps. An excellent short trail!

A tricky turn on Ricochet.

Skid Marks

Leaving skid marks. Good thing for black shorts!

Location: Drops from the top down the east side of the mountain.
Distance: 3.8 miles.
  From top to Upper Velocity: .7 miles.
  From top to Bridge The Gap: 1.8 miles.
  From top to Lincoln Express: 2.6 miles.
  From top to end at Paper Route: 3.8 miles.
Elevation: 11,000/9,040 ft.
Trail Surface: 100% singletrack.
Type of Ride: One-way downhill trail.
Terrain: Rocky; boulder-strewn ridges; low density forest, packed pumice; Mammoth Lakes & Sherwins backdrop.
Technical Level: Difficult; rocky, full-suspension-type ride.
Exertion Level: Moderate; bumpy descent requires exertion.

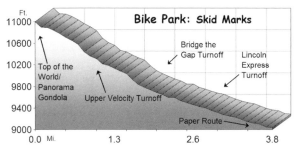

Highlights: Skid Marks is the trail to test out your suspension. As it descends from the top of Mammoth Mountain, the trail slowly morphs from a steep rocky ride to more of a smooth and gliding run near its end at Paper Route. Skid Marks exclusively provides sweeping southern vistas of the Lakes Basin surrounded by the Sierra Crest and the Sherwin Mountains. Lower on the trail, Mammoth Rock and Laurel Mountain pop into view. Various ride options abound as you drop down the mountain and pass several intersections. A lot of hardcore riders veer out at Upper Velocity while others link Bridge the Gap or Lincoln Express to get to the Bullet Downhill and tamer mid-mountain trails. But, some of the best sections of the trail are farther down as Skid Marks meets up with the Paper Route Loop.

Diving into the Mammoth Lakes basin.

Bridge The Gap

Location: Traverses the southeast side of the mountain.
Distance: 1.1 miles.
  From Brake Through to Bullet turnoff: .3 miles.
Elevation: 9650/9910 ft.
Trail Surface: 45% singletrack; 55% wide dirt road.
Type of Ride: Ridden either direction to connect trails on two sides of the mountain.
Terrain: Enormous views; backside of Lincoln Mountain.
Technical Level: Easy.
Exertion Level: Moderate/Strenuous; has a steep climb.

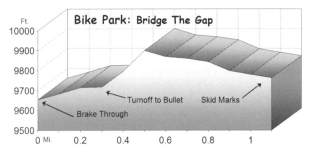

Highlights: Bridge the Gap connects Skid Marks with the mid-mountain trails, and McCoy station with the Bullet Downhill. A segment of solid singletrack climbs from Skid Marks up behind Lincoln Mountain before widening into a dirt road that descends to Bullet, Brake Through and McCoy Station. Those with a Pedal Pass who are trying to access different parts of the mountain may find this trail quite useful.

Bullet

Faster than a speeding bullet...

Location: Descends from mid-mountain to Canyon Lodge.
Distance: 1.6 miles.
Elevation: 9550/8300 ft.
Trail Surface: 100% singletrack.
Type of Ride: One-way downhiller/freeride trail.
Terrain: Forest; boulders; rocks; logs; open rock faces.
Technical Level: Very Difficult.
Exertion Level: Moderate.

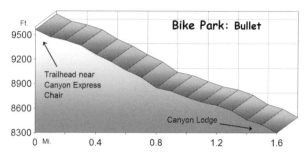

Highlights: Brimming with nonstop action, this prototypal downhill trail has seen many NORBA Racers. Seemingly endless technical sections are followed by a series of huge log drops, rock garden chutes, big drop-offs, and tight singletrack sections. The Bullet is one of the longest downhill trails on the mountain and drops about 1300 feet! For speed and adrenaline freaks, this is a must-do trail!

*There are endless opportunities to
launch some air on the Bullet.*

Big Ring

Location: Drops from Paper Route to Canyon Lodge.
Distance: 1.8 miles.
  From Paper Route to Bullet DH crossing: .5 miles.
  From Paper Route to Shotgun turnoff: .7 miles.
  From Paper Route to Canyon Lodge Parking: 1.8 miles.
Elevation: 8820/8340 ft.
Trail Surface: 100% singletrack.
Type of Ride: Ridden either up or down.
Terrain: Pine forest; ski runs; red rocks.
Technical Level: Medium.
Exertion Level: Moderate climbing; Mild descending.

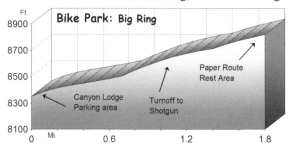

Highlights: Big Ring is a groovy trail with almost no loose pumice. Its easy to keep a steady pace whether you are climbing or descending on this trail. The trail descends from the Paper Route rest area and crosses the Bullet Downhill trail, the turnoff to Shotgun, and the Warming Wall rock climbing area before ending at the Canyon Lodge Parking area. To reach the Bike Park Shuttle, keep riding straight down Canyon Blvd to The Village At Mammoth.

Lincoln Express

Location: Traversing across Lincoln Mountain.
Distance: 1 mile.
  From Skid Marks to Bullet DH: .8 miles.
  From Bullet DH to Brake Through: .2 miles.
Elevation: 9410/9220 ft.
Trail Surface: 100% singletrack.
Type of Ride: Ridden either direction.
Terrain: Mountainside; southeastern views; open forest.
Technical Level: Easy/Medium.
Exertion Level: Moderate; some climbing.

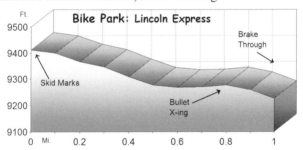

Highlights: This tight and somewhat-rocky singletrack skirts the steep slope of Lincoln Mountain. Lincoln Express is a scenic and fun way to cut across the mountain to access other trails; most commonly connecting Skid Marks to Brake Through or Bullet. A couple nice tree roots and small rock jumps add some zest to an excellent trail.

Lincoln Express skirts Lincoln Mountain with fantastic views.

Shotgun

Overcoming the pucker factor on the Shotgun log ride.

Location: Drops from Downtown to Canyon Lodge.
Distance: 1 mile.
Elevation: 8813/8400 ft.
Trail Surface: 100% singletrack.
Type of Ride: Ridden downhill; freeride-type trail.
Terrain: Pine Forest; logs; rocks; jumps.
Technical Level: Difficult.
Exertion Level: Moderate; some uphill.

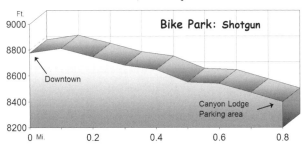

Highlights: Shotgun commences with an uphill jaunt before transforming into a killer downhill trail! Various freeriding characteristics such as drop-offs, jumps, and log rides spice it up. Like one long X-Zone, this trail is a blast!

Airing out on Shotgun.

Paper Route

Location: Off Downtown Trail, below Brake Through trail.
Distance: 5.4 mile loop.
  Upper trailhead off Downtown to X-Zone: .2 miles.
  Upper trailhead off Downtown to Big Ring: .8 miles.
  Upper trailhead off Downtown to Timber Ridge: 1.4 miles.
  Upper trailhead off Downtown to Lakes Trail: 1.5 miles.
  Upper trailhead off Downtown to Juniper: 2.3 miles.
  Upper trailhead off Downtown to Skid Marks: 3.4 miles.
  Upper trailhead to Lower trailhead at Downtown: 5.4 miles.
Elevation: 8760/9040 ft.
Trail Surface: 100% singletrack.
Type of Ride: Directional loop with two offshoot sections.
Terrain: Dense pine forest; exposed ski runs; great views.
Technical Level: Easy; with occasional rocky sections.
Exertion Level: Moderate; some gradual climbing.

Best paper route on the planet!

Highlights: There is something for all riders on this packed singletrack. The full loop will appeal to those who want some moderate uphill riding, while many others will simply ride down from Skid Marks or Downtown. The Bullet DH crosses two sections of the trail. Big Ring, Timber Ridge, and Juniper all drop from different segments of Paper Route. Most of Paper Route is twisty and smooth, with a few rocky sections. Two segments of Paper Route traverse across the mountain to/from Downtown trail; an X-Zone with excellent jumps drops between these two trails. A popular rest area with drink-

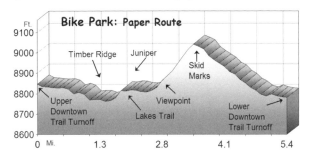

ing water is located at the intersection of Paper Route and Big Ring. Paper Route connects to so many other ridable trails, that it can be used in many creative cross-country loops.

Pedaling some of the smoothest and tackiest singletrack in the park.

Timber Ridge

Location: Drops from Paper Route to Juniper.
Distance: .9 miles.
Elevation: 8760/8600 ft.
Trail Surface: 100% singletrack.

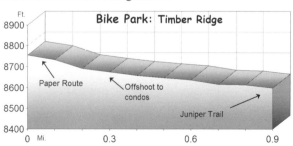

Type of Ride: Ridden both downhill or uphill.
Terrain: Pine and fir forest; open ski runs.
Technical Level: Easy/Medium.
Exertion Level: Mild riding downhill; Moderate riding uphill.

Highlights: Timber Ridge provides an alternative means to bypass part of Paper Route if you are going down to Juniper Springs/Eagle Express area. This trail glides through forested areas with a few good berms to carve up.

Juniper

Making summer S-turns on the Juniper trail.

Location: Connecting Paper Route and Eagle/Juniper Lodge.
Distance: 1.9 miles.
Elevation: 8800/8100 ft.
Trail Surface: 100% singletrack.
Type of Ride: Usually ridden downhill from Paper Route.
Terrain: Pine & fir forest; lush spring area; wild flowers.

Technical Level: Medium/Difficult.
Exertion Level: Moderate.

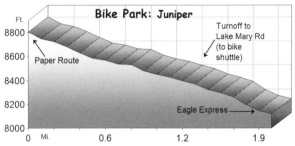

Highlights: Juniper is simply one of the most fun sections of trail on the mountain. At a moderately steep pace, Juniper slaloms its way through an endless series of turns with various small rock and tree root dropoffs. After passing the turnoff to Lake Mary and the Bike Shuttle, a lush new singletrack has replaced the harsh ski-run switchbacks. The rest of this trail snakes its way into a grassy dense forest of wildflowers, aspens and fir, across a series of bridges, and on to the Eagle Express/Juniper Lodge area. Most riders will love jamming on this fast and rhythmic trail!

Lakes Trail

Location: Connects Twin Lakes with Paper Route.
Distance: 1.2 miles.
  From Twin Lakes to Juniper Trail: .6 miles.
Elevation: 8730/8570 ft.
Trail Surface: 100% singletrack (somewhat wide at first).
Type of Ride: Ridden either direction to connect Mammoth Mountain trails with Panorama Dome/Mammoth Rock Trails.
Terrain: Steep hillside; aspen trees; fir and pine trees; Sierra Crest; Twin Lakes; waterfalls; Mammoth Creek views.

Another mountain bike picture.

Technical Level: Easy/Medium.
Exertion Level: Moderate.

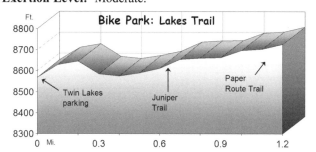

Highlights: Meandering in and out of sunny open areas and forested ski runs, this trail ascends from Twin Lakes to Juniper Trail and beyond to the Paper Route loop. As you pedal this fantastic trail, you'll be serenaded by a cascading waterfall, as Mammoth Creek descends into the canyon below Twin Lakes. A myriad of visual delights fill the ride as you look down the Mammoth Creek Canyon toward Crowley Lake and the White Mountains. You'll also see splendid views of the town, Glass Mountains, the Sierra Crest, Twin Lakes, Panorama Dome area, and Laurel Mountain. Beware of a sketchy hairpin turn on the steep slope about a quarter mile up from Twin Lakes! To reach the bike shuttle from this trail, descend Lake Mary Road and then turn left on Canyon Blvd.

Proposed Trails

Mammoth Mountain is always improving and striving to expand the bike park. Depending on several factors, such as the environmental approval process by the Forest Service, some new trails may be added. Proposed trails near Chair 4 include "Pipeline," "Flow," "DC-10," and the "Ridge Trail" near Chair 12.

In 2005, two new freeride trail areas have been approved and will be built during the summer bike season. The "Twilight Zone" off of Chain Smoke will add even more thrills to this area of the mountain. Likewise, the "Kamikaze Park" will add more fun for the freeride-minded bikers! Yeehaa!

Racing the NORBA US Downhill Championships on Upper Velocity.

Mammoth Area Trails

Trails, apart from the Bike Park, in and around the town of Mammoth Lakes

Uptown/Downtown Loop

Swoopy singletrack on Downtown Trail.

Location: From North Village to the Earthquake Fault.
Distance: 4.3 miles.
Elevation: 8060/8500 ft.
Trail Surface: 100% singletrack.
Type of Ride: Loop.
Terrain: Fir forest; Earthquake Fault; parallels HWY 203.
Technical Level: Easy/Medium.
Exertion Level: Moderate.

Highlights: Uptown and Downtown trails are both a local and tourist favorite, as they are the most accessible singletrack in the Mammoth area. This popular loop curves and rolls its way up to the "Earthquake Fault" area at a moderate pitch before descending back down to the Village. This ride consists of the lower Non-Bike Park segment of the full Downtown/Uptown trails, and is open for free public use. Riding farther up the trails officially brings you into the Bike Park, which requires a Bike Park pass.

Options: This ride can be extended by buying a Mammoth Mountain Bike Park pass, or by heading up the Mountain View Trail near the Earthquake Fault. (See Ride 3). Also, half way up, riders can cross HWY 203 and take the Scenic Loop Trail (Ride 10).

Note: Ride Uptown going uphill (closest to HWY 203) and Downtown while descending (farther from HWY 203). Be prepared to see plenty of other riders in peak summer months.

Directions/Access: In Mammoth Lakes, head up HWY 203 (Main St) to North Village. The trailhead is on the left, just past the intersection of HWY 203 and Forest Trail Road.

Climbing Uptown Trail.

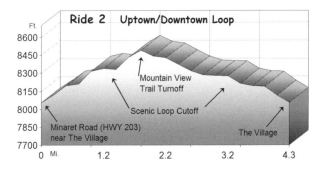

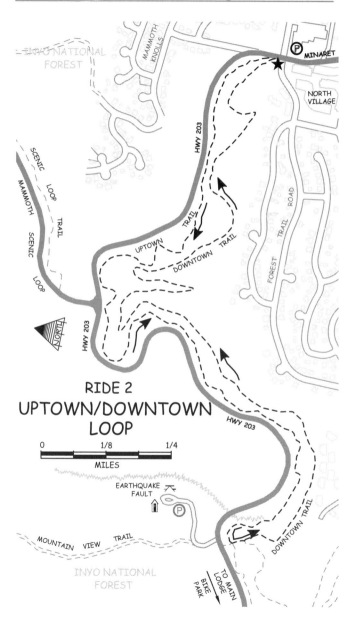

MAMMOTH KNOLLS

INYO NATIONAL FOREST

P MINARET

NORTH VILLAGE

HWY 203

FOREST TRAIL ROAD

SCENIC LOOP TRAIL

MAMMOTH SCENIC LOOP

UPTOWN TRAIL

DOWNTOWN TRAIL

NORTH

HWY 203

RIDE 2
UPTOWN/DOWNTOWN
LOOP

0   1/8   1/4
MILES

EARTHQUAKE FAULT

P

HWY 203

DOWNTOWN TRAIL

MOUNTAIN VIEW TRAIL

INYO NATIONAL FOREST

TO MAIN LODGE

BIKE PARK

Mileage Guide

0.0	The trailhead is on the west side of HWY 203. You'll see 2 trails; take Uptown, which is the rightmost.
0.9	After a large switchback, you'll reach a wide flat open-area. Continue on up the trail. [Another option is to take the Scenic Loop trail (leading toward Inyo Craters) by heading right and crossing HWY 203. See Ride 10 for more detail].
1.9	Four-way junction! A large tree on the left has a bike symbol sign marking the intersection. Go left on the connector trail, which will soon merge left again onto the Downtown Trail. In the summer, a large Bike Park sign signifies the necessity of a park pass to continue up the Uptown Trail (See Ride 1K). The trail to the right links Uptown with the Mountain View Trail; it crosses the HWY and continues all the way to Minaret Vista (see Ride 3).
3.0	Keep riding on the main trail as you pass through the wide open-area once again. [A 90 degree left turn leads to the Scenic Loop Trail and Ride 10].
4.3	Trail ends back at HWY 203.

In the summer, signs mark the end of the free public access boundary of Uptown and Downtown trails at a four way inter-section. The loop continues to the left. Going right across HWY 203 links up with the Mountain View Trail.

Mountain View Trail

Seeing the forest through the trees.

Location: Connects the "Earthquake Fault" to Minaret Summit.

Distance: 11 miles round trip (more possible with exploration).

Elevation: 8500/9130 ft.

Trail Surface: 52% singletrack; 48% dirt/jeep road.

Type of Ride: Out & Back.

Terrain: Forest; pumice meadows; creeks; mountain views.

Technical Level: Medium.

Exertion Level: Moderate/Strenuous; gradual climbing with some steeper sections.

Highlights: Mountain View is a vintage Mammoth trail that intermingles some epic singletrack with narrow dirt (packed pumice) roads. It starts at the turnoff to the ill-named "Earthquake Fault," which really is a seismic fissure. Hidden deep in a Lodgepole and Jeffrey pine forest, this trail gradually finds its way up to the unforgettable lookout at Minaret Summit. Don't miss this classic ride!

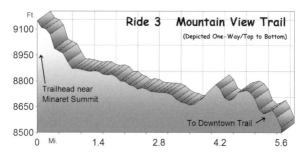

Options: There are several additions that make for a longer ride. Rides 2 (Uptown/Downtown Loop), 4 (San Joaquin Ridge/Hard Core), and 5 (Starkweather Trail), are commonly combined with Mountain View trail.

If you have a bike park pass, a great loop can also be made by adding the Beach Cruiser and Mountain View Trails in the Mammoth Mountain Bike Park.

Enjoying the "secluded" forest singletrack.

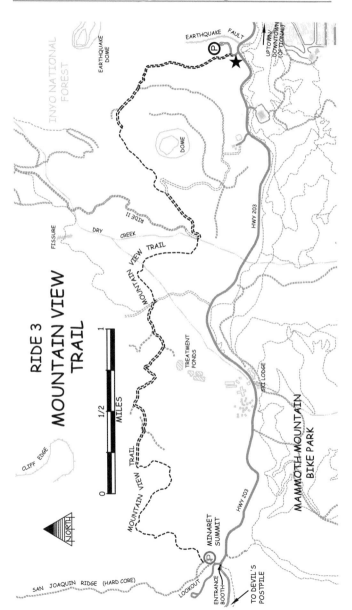

RIDE 3
MOUNTAIN VIEW
TRAIL

<u>Downtown/Uptown Addition:</u> Most Mammoth locals will combine Mountain View Trail with the Uptown and Downtown trails. By adding some superb singletrack, this makes a 15.5 mile ride from The Village. Ride Uptown Trail 1.9 miles to a split with a sign "Mt View/Hard Core." Turn right and cross HWY 203 and ride a short distance to the Mountain View trailhead on the Earthquake Fault road. When returning, cross HWY 203 and take Downtown trail (just beyond Uptown trail) back down to the village.

<u>San Joaquin Ridge (Hard Core) Addition:</u> At the top of Mountain View Trail, turn right on the dirt road and follow this as it steeply scales the San Joaquin Ridge. Hard Core is a physically demanding out & back that will add about 5.4 tough miles to the ride. The endless panoramic views are energizing, however. See Ride 4 for further details.

Note: Many roads split off of the main route, however, the trail intersections are usually marked with a biker symbol tag on the trees.

Directions/Access: From Mammoth Lakes, drive or ride up HWY 203 past North Village toward Mammoth Mountain.

Turn right at the Earthquake Fault and drive to the parking lot. The trailhead is about 150 feet back down the paved road (toward HWY 203) and on the right between some logs. A confirming sign is posted just ahead on the trail/road.

Mountain View madness.

Mileage Guide	
0.0	From the trailhead near the Earthquake Fault, start riding up the trail/road. Stay straight on the main route, ignoring the many remnants of old dirt roads that split off.
1.0	Veer left, staying on the main trail/road.
1.3	Prepare for a mega steep and deep pumice climb! Most mere mortals may have to settle for a quick hike 'n' bike section. After this climb the road turns to singletrack, and winds its way along a ridge with excellent tree-framed views of Pumice Flat, Deer Mountain, White Wing, Two Teats, and San Joaquin Ridge.
1.6	When you reach a major dirt road; go right and downhill.
2.0	At the bottom, turn left onto the signed trail and cross over Dry Creek on a couple of small bridges.
2.8	Go right on the road. Just ahead, pedal left at the signed split and keep going straight past any offshoot roads.
3.1	Split ahead! Go right on the pumice dirt road; a "No Snowmobiles" sign is just beyond.
3.6	Pedal past the spur roads off to the right.
3.8	Split; go right on the trail.
4.1	After riding through a pumice flat, the trail climbs up into the forest where a sign marks the final all-single-track leg of the climb. The cardio action will start to pick up a bit from now on.
5.5	The trail ends at an open dirt parking area. Going Right on the dirt road leads to Ride 4, San Joaquin Ridge (Hard Core). Not far to the left, the road leads to several options: HWY 203, the Red's Meadow entrance booth, trailhead to Starkweather Trail (Ride 5), and the turnoff to Minaret Summit. The viewpoint of Minaret Summit is the perfect excuse to take a break. The rest of the ride is an out & back; return the way you came.
11.0	Back at the bottom.

San Joaquin Ridge Ride
(Hard Core)

On top of the Sierra world!

Location: Climbs San Joaquin Ridge above Minaret Summit.

Distance: 5.4 miles round trip.

Elevation: 9150/10,240 ft.

Trail Surface: 100% jeep/dirt road/doubletrack.

Type of Ride: Out & Back.

Terrain: Extensive panoramic views ; early summer wildflowers; exposed open pumice areas with occasional pine trees.

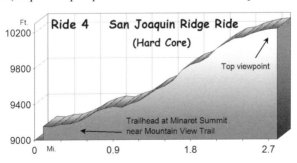

The San Joaquin Ridge is hard core scenic.

Technical Level: Medium/Difficult; some steep and rutted sections on somewhat loose soil.

Exertion Level: Very Strenuous; mega leg burner especially if you ride up Mountain View Trail first.

Highlights: The sightseeing and intense cardio workout are the main draws of this one. The views extend from nearby Mammoth Mountain, the rugged Ritter Range, the San Joaquin rift, June Mountain, White Wing Mountain, the Headwaters of Owens River, Mono Craters, the entire Long Valley Caldera, Crowley Lake and the White Mountains. Once you emerge from the forest, it will seem as though you have entered a new realm, leaving all the chaos and stress of humanity below. This ride will make you ponder the secrets of the universe, and how such a resplendent land was formed for us to play in! If you have never been up here, its time to realign priorities and do it!

Options: Combinations with Mammoth Mountain Trails and/or, Mountain View Trail (Ride 3) will make a longer ride.

<u>Ultra-Mega Mammoth Ride Option:</u> Ride from town to the top of San Joaquin Ridge! Take Uptown (Ride 2) to Mountain View (Ride 3) to Hard Core and back down via the Downtown Trail. This will make a tough 21-mile ride. If you have a spirit of invincibility (and extra energy bars), tack on Starkweather

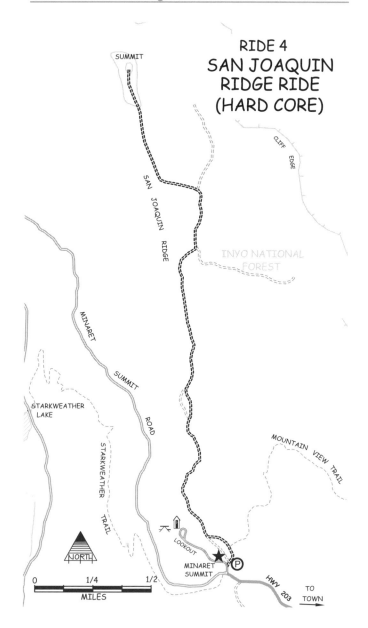

RIDE 4
SAN JOAQUIN
RIDGE RIDE
(HARD CORE)

SUMMIT

CLIFF EDGE

SAN JOAQUIN RIDGE

INYO NATIONAL FOREST

MINARET SUMMIT ROAD

STARKWEATHER LAKE

STARKWEATHER TRAIL

MOUNTAIN VIEW TRAIL

LOOKOUT

MINARET SUMMIT

HWY 203

TO TOWN

NORTH

0   1/4   1/2
MILES

Trail (Ride 5 - open offseason only) for a 28 mile ride with more than 3500 vertical feet of high altitude climbing. Accomplishing this will surely give you supreme feelings of indefatigable glory and indomitable pride as you look back on all that vast terrain you just conquered!

Note: This is high altitude riding; be prepared for thin air.

Directions/Access: From Mammoth Lakes, take HWY 203 (Main Street in town) all the way past Mammoth Mountain and up to Minaret Summit. Just before the main entrance booth to Devil's Postpile, turn right on the dirt road and park in the open pullout area just ahead. Start biking up this road, designated by USFS as "Hard Core." The trailhead is also accessed by Mountain View Trail (Ride 3).

Mileage Guide	
0.0	Pedal up the road, north of the dirt parking area.
.10	Pass the top of Mountain View Trailhead on the right.
.40	You'll notice a sign depicting the bike ride at the circular round-about.
.80	The road splits here. Take either side, as they will soon come back together.
1.7	The route curves left as a road comes in from the right. Prepare for a super steep granny gear session ahead!
2.0	At the split, stay left as you come to another very steep section. Just ahead the awesome scenery will intensify!
2.7	Top! Enjoy that endorphin high! Return down the same way.
5.4	Back at dirt parking area.

The San Joaquin Ridge 4x4 route.

Starkweather Trail
(off-season only)

Sometimes it feels like you are floating on this trail.

Location: Descends from Minaret Summit to Starkweather Lake behind Mammoth Mountain.

Distance: 6.8-mile loop with road; 2.6 miles one-way.

Elevation: 9150/8040 ft.

Trail Surface: 100% singletrack.

Type of Ride: Loop or Out & Back.

Terrain: Red fir and pine forest; mountain views; Red's Meadow area; numerous creeks with small waterfalls in the spring.

Technical Level: Medium/Difficult; fairly steep.

Exertion Level: Strenuous; steep climb back up the road.

Highlights: Starkweather trail is one of Mammoth's most recent trails open to bikers! Although it is closed to biking during the peak summer and fall months (while Red's Meadow

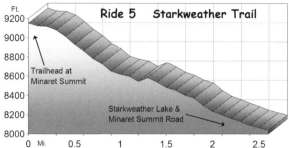

Shuttle is running), it is well worth the wait! At a relatively steep pace, this euphoric downhill thrill is mostly smooth packed pumice with drainage swales and small drops to spice it up! As you descend, classic Minaret views rise through a lush forest filled with many small creeks. You'll pass the remains of a mining cabin from the early 1900's. Then the trail follows a stream into a gorgeous meadow with wildflowers and wanders down to the trout-filled Starkweather lake. You might want to bring a fishing pole, as there are some Big Ones in there!

Options: If you don't mind riding pavement, there is a lot to explore in the Red's Meadow area (to the left when you come to Minaret Summit Road near the lake). Another option is to ride as an out & back; just remember it's a steep climb back up! For a much longer ride, see below:

Climbing up from Starkweather Lake.

Steep winding turns fill up this fun trail!

<u>Village to Starkweather Option:</u> The ultimate cross-country (and much more demanding) 23-mile version of this ride begins near the Village at Mammoth. Pedal Uptown to Mountain View Trail and then down Starkweather Trail, back up Minaret Summit Road to Mountain View Trail (or ride to Beach Cruiser on Mammoth Mountain) and descend to Downtown trail. (See Rides 2 & 3).

Note: When the Red's Meadow shuttle bus (fees required) is running, approximately from mid-June through October, bikes are not allowed on this trail. Many hikers/backpackers utilize this trail in the summer. Bike it only in Spring and late Fall!

Directions/Access: From Mammoth Lakes, drive up HWY 203 all the way past Mammoth Mountain and on to Minaret Vista. Park above the Red's Meadow/Devil's Postpile Entrance Booth in the parking lot to the right. The trail commences across the road just below the entrance booth. The trail can also be accessed from Mountain View Trail (Ride 3), or from Beach Cruiser to Mountain View Trail (Ride 1B/C).

Mileage Guide	
0.0	The trail starts near the Minaret Vista entrance booth. Take this and prepare for action as the trail drops 1,100 fun feet in elevation!

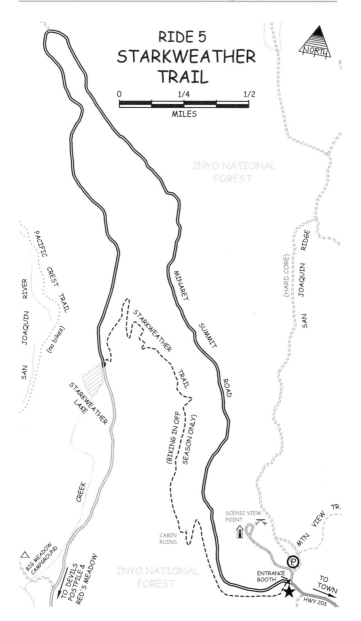

RIDE 5
STARKWEATHER
TRAIL

NORTH

0   1/4   1/2
MILES

INYO NATIONAL FOREST

PACIFIC CREST TRAIL
(no bikes)

SAN JOAQUIN RIVER

STARKWEATHER LAKE

STARKWEATHER TRAIL

(BIKING IN OFF SEASON ONLY)

MINARET SUMMIT ROAD

SAN JOAQUIN RIDGE
(HARD CORE)

CREEK

CABIN RUINS

SCENIC VIEW POINT

MTN. VIEW TR.

BIG MEADOW CAMPGROUND

TO DEVILS POSTPILE & RED'S MEADOW

INYO NATIONAL FOREST

ENTRANCE BOOTH

P

TO TOWN

HWY 203

| 2.6 | After descending some wooden steps, the trail emerges onto Minaret Summit Road across from Starkweather Lake. If you are riding this as a loop, turn right on Minaret Summit Road after exploring the area. This paved road passes several creeks and awe-inspiring viewpoints as you climb back up to the summit. |
| 6.8 | Pass the trailhead and entrance booth, ride on to the parking area or to your final destination. |

Mammoth Rock Trail

Carving tracks of a different kind at the base of the famed Sherwins.

Location: Traverses the lower Sherwins; Mammoth Lakes.
Distance: 2.7 miles one-way; 6 mile loop with roads.
Elevation: 7860/8460 ft.
Trail Surface: 100% singletrack.

Type of Ride: Loop, One-Way shuttle, or Out & Back.
Terrain: Sherwin Mountains; Mammoth Rock; views from Mammoth Mountain to Crowley Lake; forest; sagebrush; boulders; steep mountainside.
Technical Level: Medium.
Exertion Level: Moderate.

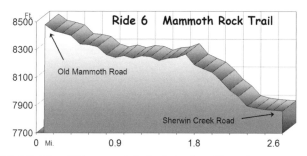

Highlights: This groovin' singletrack will conjure up sensations of ecstasy as it soars across the vertically exposed face of the Sherwins! Mammoth Rock, a massive limestone and marble monolith, is an interesting geological feature near the upper trailhead. It is one of the last remains of the primordial ocean floor that eroded while the mountains were uplifted under it. After passing Mammoth Rock, segments of the trail will teeter along the side of the steep boulder slope, making for great views! The trail gets a bit sandy toward the bottom, where horse-use has pulverized the soil into fine grains of sand. Fortunately, the trail is steep enough to barge through it.

Options: Most people ride a loop from town, by riding up bike paths and/or Old Mammoth Road and on to the trailhead (See Map). To add more dirt to the loop, ride through the meadow trails behind the borrow pit off of Sherwin Creek Road (see "Other Riding In The Area: Meadow Trails" below).

Some downhiller-types shuttle it by dropping a car at Sherwin creek road. It can also be ridden as an out & back from Sherwin Creek Road, although, the first section riding up the trail is very sandy.

An excellent longer option, is to ride from town and combine the trail with Panorama Dome Loop (Ride 8).

Note: Be Aware! This is a multi-use trail, with horse-riders and a lot of hikers and joggers. Please help keep this trail open to bikes by being respectful and yielding to other users.

Bunny-hopping through the rabbit brush!

Directions/Access: From Mammoth Lakes, drive up Old Mammoth Road to trailheads:

To ride as a loop, ride to/park at Mammoth Creek Park on Old Mammoth Road (about .8 miles from 203/Main Street).

The upper trailhead is located about 2.5 miles past Mammoth Creek Park on Old Mammoth Road. After the road steepens and makes a sharp left turn, look for the trailhead/parking pull-out on the left.

To start at the lower trailhead, take a left on Sherwin Creek Road (just beyond and across from the park on Old Mammoth Road), and ride/drive .7 miles. The trailhead is on the right.

Mileage Guide	
0.0	If you are riding as a loop from town, ride up Old Mammoth Road to the trailhead; see Options & Directions/Access above. Look for the wooden sign at the trailhead on upper Old Mammoth Road and get ready for fun! (An alternative entry is .20 miles farther up Old Mammoth Road on the left. A singletrack descends and merges in just above the trailhead).

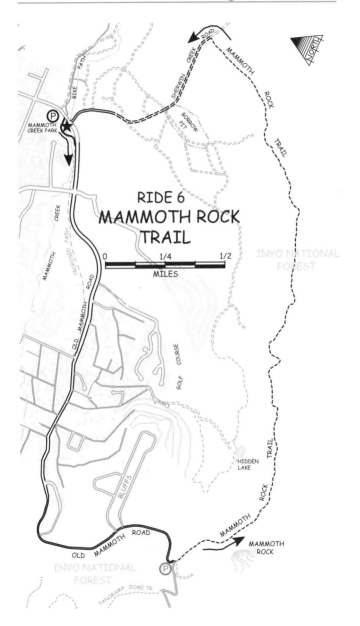

RIDE 6
MAMMOTH ROCK
TRAIL

1.3	The ride will now lead away from the steeper slopes and head into the forest.
1.7	Suddenly, the trail drops into more of a desert environment. Ignore the horse trails that spur off the main trail.
2.7	Sherwin Creek Road. To finish the loop turn left and ride the dirt road about .7 miles back to Old Mammoth Road. If you started at Mammoth Creek Park, it is just across the street and to the right.

Other Riding Nearby

A. Mammoth Creek Area

Several dirt roads on either side of Mammoth Creek receive their fair share of bike tracks, especially when there is snow on the higher trails. Mammoth Creek Park on Old Mammoth

A symbol of Old Mammoth - an original 19th century pelton wheel from the mining days.

Road is a great staging area for exploring the area. Both Sherwin Creek Road and the dirt road "3S09" descend on either side of the creek across Old Mammoth Road from the Park. These roads, along with a plethora of spurs and splits, can be ridden in various sized loops. There is plenty to explore while pedaling out a great workout. The open desert meadows are flanked by the Sherwin range, while many of the cooler forested areas hide ancient lava flows. Since aspen trees thickly line Mammoth Creek, biking the area during peak fall colors makes for one picturesque ride.

Less than a mile from civilization, but away from it all.

B. Meadow Trails

A few singletrack trails and doubletrack wind around the meadow area below Mammoth Rock. Primarily used by the local residents, these trails wind through meadows and over small creeks. A trail passes through aspen and Lodgepole pine groves on it's way to the little-known Hidden Lake. This is a local horse riding area, and some of the trails get quite bumpy.

While not a mountain bike destination by itself, some people utilize these trails and roads in creating a loop with Mammoth Rock Trail. Dirt roads converge behind the borrow pit on Sherwin Creek Road (in between Old Mammoth Road and the Mammoth Rock lower trailhead) and lead into the meadow area near the golf course. One trail connects to Tamarack Street, a side street off of Old Mammoth Road.

Panorama Dome Trail

*Frolicking on the Panorama Dome Trail, with
Dragons Tail in the background.*

Location: Between Old Mammoth and Twin Lakes.
Distance: 2 miles.
Elevation: 8520/8640 ft.
Trail Surface: 99% singletrack; 1% paved road.
Type of Ride: Loop with Out & Back section.
Terrain: Pine, fir, and aspen trees; views of Mammoth Rock,
Sierra Crest, Juniper Ridge, and Mammoth Mountain.
Technical Level: Medium.
Exertion Level: Moderate.

Highlights: Also known as "Vista Trail," this little stash of
whirling singletrack is a true gem for the mountain bike crowd.
Fun for all levels of bikers, the trail flows in and out of a dense

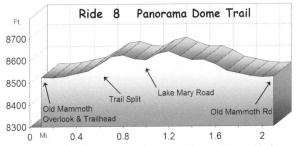

forest on the side of Panorama Dome. The trail itself is in great condition with tacky soil and nothing too steep. This version of the loop seems to maximize fun downhill sections.

Also of note is the area's historical importance. After the split in the trails, a wide ditch nearby conveyed water from Mammoth Creek for the Mammoth Mine stamp mill. This flume dates back to 1868. The original wild west town of Mammoth City was located in the area surrounding the trailhead. Not far below the trailhead, a hiking trail (no bikes) leads down to the giant stamp mill ruins.

Options: The Panorama Dome Trail is in a perfect location for connecting Lake Mary Road and Old Mammoth Road with other rides. To lengthen the ride, tack on the Mammoth Rock Trail (see below), Horseshoe Lake Loop (Ride 9) and/or the Lakes Trail on Mammoth Mountain (Ride 1Y).

<u>Panorama Dome/Mammoth Rock Combo:</u>   Connecting the Panorama Dome Ride with the Mammoth Rock Trail makes for an awesome 8.5 mile loop. Pedal up to Panorama Dome from town and then hit the

S-turn diversion.

PAPER ROUTE

BIKE PARK

LAKE MARY ROAD

TO TOWN

NORTH

MAMMOTH CREEK

LAKES TRAIL

RIDE 8
PANORAMA DOME
TRAIL

0   1/8   1/4

MILES

VIEW POINT

PANORAMA   DOME   TRAIL

TWIN LAKES

MAMMOTH   ROAD

OLD

INYO NATIONAL FOREST

PANORAMA DOME

LAKE MARY ROAD

WATER TANK

RUINS

HIKING TR

OLD   MAMMOTH   ROAD
(MILL ST)

MAMMOTH ROCK TRAIL

Mammoth Rock Trail (Ride 6) on the way back down.

Note: There are other trails on the dome, but most are frequently used by horsemen and are not very suitable (or open) for bike use. One trail across from Twin Lakes is disappearing, but follows part of Mammoth Creek and the flume before veering off to a dramatic lookout on a sheer cliff above the town of Mammoth Lakes and the Valentine Reserve.

Setting off on the Panorama Dome Trail.

Directions/Access: Ride or drive up Old Mammoth Road in Mammoth Lakes. The trailhead is about 3.5 miles up Old Mammoth Road from Main St/HWY 203; (only a quarter mile beyond the Mammoth Rock Trailhead). An overlook and small pullout are at the trailhead.

Mileage Guide	
0.0	The trailhead is at the Old Mammoth overlook; showcasing Mammoth Knolls, Crowley Lake, and Mammoth Rock. Ride into the forest, passing a huge rock outcropping on the left.

.50	The trail splits here; go left! Nearby are the remains of the stamp mill water flume from the late 1800's.
.80	Soon, you will come to Lake Mary Road. Turn right and ride for 100 feet before turning right once again to catch the next section of trail.
1.5	When you return to the original split, stay left and continue down the initial segment.
2.0	Old Mammoth Road trailhead/viewpoint.

Horseshoe Lake Trail

Horseshoe lake reflecting the backside of Mammoth Mountain.

Location: Mammoth Lakes Basin.
Distance: 1.7 miles.
Elevation: 8890/8950 ft.
Trail Surface: 90% singletrack; 10% old dirt road.
Type of Ride: Loop.

Terrain: High alpine lakes; dense forest; granite outcroppings; numerous creeks.

Technical Level: Easy.

Exertion Level: Mild.

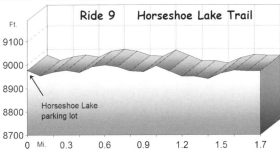

Highlights: Horseshoe Lake Trail, also known as "Water Wheel Trail," is a superb cruiser-type ride on the only legal singletrack in the lakes basin! Most of this easy trail is in a thick pine forest, and crosses over creeks several times. Beautiful views of the lakes framed by the Sierra Crest and the backside of Mammoth Mountain add to this high alpine loop. Also, you'll notice that this is one of the quietest areas in the lakes basin since no motor boats are buzzing around.

Options: Near the end of the ride, a trail cuts off to the right, leading around to the Lake Mary outlet. A lot of bikers check this trail out, but its not an "official" bike trail. For more mileage, add in Panorama Dome Loop (Ride 8).

Note: Stay off the Mammoth Pass Trail, which leads into Wilderness. You'll also want to avoid the profusely abundant horse packer trails in the area, which appear as trenches of annihilated pumice and horse poop. You might find yourself wondering

Just behind: a parking lot full of SUVs.

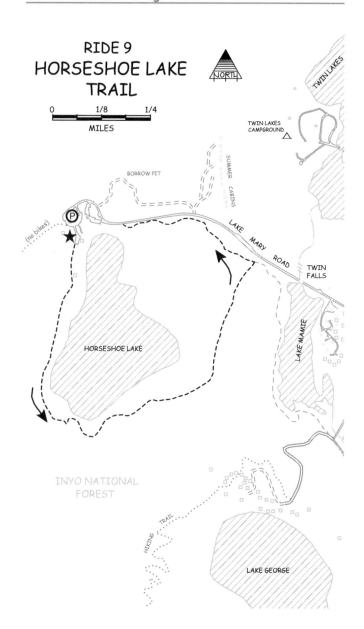

RIDE 9
HORSESHOE LAKE
TRAIL

NORTH

0   1/8   1/4
MILES

TWIN LAKES

TWIN LAKES
CAMPGROUND

BORROW PIT

SUMMER CABINS

(no bikes)

P

LAKE MARY ROAD

TWIN
FALLS

HORSESHOE LAKE

LAKE MAMIE

INYO NATIONAL
FOREST

HIKING TRAIL

LAKE GEORGE

Feelin' the groove.

how only one trail in this entire area is legal for mountain bikes. But at least there's one!

Also, note that there is a CO_2 hazard area near the trailhead (not associated with all the SUVs). You will certainly see signs describing this phenomenon. Evidence of dead pine trees attests to the presence of the gas seeping from the south side of the volcano, Mammoth Mountain. The CO_2 pools in depressions near the tree-till areas; do not linger in these areas.

Directions/Access: From the town of Mammoth Lakes, drive up Main Street and continue as it becomes Lake Mary Road. Take this all the way to its end at Horseshoe lake and park in the oversize parking lot.

Mileage Guide	
0.0	To ride the lake counter-clockwise, pass the bathrooms on the north side of the lake. You will see a MAMBO sign depicting the trail. The pavement will turn into a dirt road, which soon narrows into singletrack.
.20	Stay to the left, as a closed road veers off here.
.50	Keep riding past the rock climbing trails off to the right.
.70	Pedal through the burned down remnants of old cabins.
1.0	As you ride, you will pass by perpendicular horse trails. Ignore these. The next section of trail will become more road-like, but will soon narrow back down.
1.2	Just before reaching Lake Mary Road, go left on the trail that parallels the paved road. (This is across from the trail that leads to Lake Maime Lake to the right).
1.6	The trail ends near Lake Mary Road and the Horseshoe parking lot. Ride along the dirt shoulder and then cut across the dirt parking lot back to the start.
1.7	Circle complete.

Scenic Loop-Trail Ride

Location: Between HWY 203 and the Inyo Craters.
Distance: 6.7 miles. (9.2 miles with Uptown/Downtown).
Elevation: 8050/8400 ft.
Trail Surface: 33% singletrack/mx trails; 61% narrow dirt road; 4% graded dirt road; 2% paved road.
Type of Ride: Loop, with Out & Back section.
Terrain: Fir & pine forest; Dry Creek; mountain views.

Climbing the Scenic Loop Trail near the junction with Uptown.

Technical Level: Medium/Difficult; some segments with loose soil, deep pumice, rocks, and short steep hills.
Exertion Level: Moderate; with a few short strenuous sections.

Highlights: The Scenic Loop-Trail Ride is a great all-around ride that circumnavigates a portion of the paved Mammoth Scenic Loop Road. While much of the ride is on loose energy-sucking pumice, there is plenty of fun to be had. This cross-country style trail has both fast and furious descents and a challenging climb back up. This ride is conveniently located for linking to many other nearby trails.

Options: Most people ride this trail from Mammoth via the Uptown/Downtown Loop (Ride 2). For a very fun and longer ride combine this with the Dry Creek Loop (Ride 11), Inyo Craters Singletrack (Ride 12), and/or The Mammoth Knolls Loop (Ride 15).

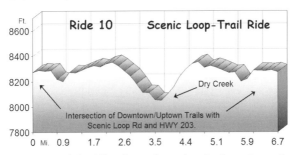

Note: Some of the bike signs along the singletrack portion of the ride are labeled "Inyo Craters." This ride is the way to get to the original non-motorized Inyo Craters Singletrack (Ride 12).

Also, note that the condition of the trails and roads here can change dramatically depending on the type of users. Sometimes 4-wheeled OHVs (ATVs) and trucks drive on the trails and ruin them. Unfortunately, some of the best sections of singletrack have been widened by a large increase in ATV use in the last couple years. Also, the Forest Service recently clear-cut much of the area along the Scenic Loop Road, which added to truck traffic in the trail area. The best way to preserve singletrack in the area is for mountain bikers to continue riding these trails as much as possible to help re-establish a "single" track.

Directions/Access: From the North Village area in Mammoth, take 203 to the intersection of Mammoth Scenic Loop Road. The ride starts on the right-hand side of the Scenic Loop Road, about 300 feet up from HWY 203. There are limited turnouts and dirt roads off the side to park at. Better yet, ride the Uptown/Downtown trails from the North Village area; a sign labeled "to Inyo Craters" marks the way to the trailhead.

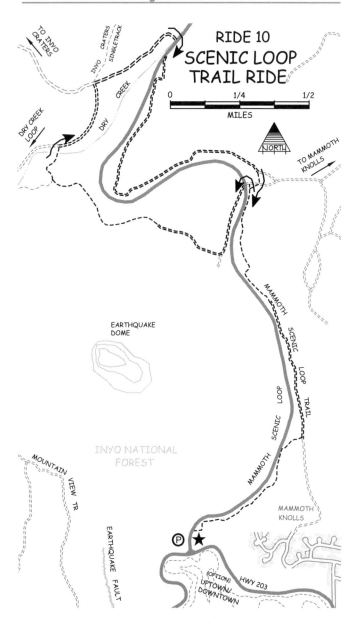

Racing the wind.

Mileage Guide	
0.0	From the HWY 203/Scenic Loop Road intersection, ride up the Scenic Loop Road a little way and find the trail (more like a dirt road at first) on the right. A small sign says "to Inyo Craters." It will become more of a bermed-out and pumicey motorcycle trail soon.
.50	Merge onto the dirt road.
.60	Veer left on the dirt OHV road at the left-hand curve, and endure some sandier riding for a while. Eventually it will narrow into a trail again.
1.7	The trail ends as it reaches a perpendicular road. Go left by crossing the Scenic Loop Road (paved) and continue down the other side on a dirt road that veers left.
2.0	Go right up the road.
2.1	Once again, go right, then up a steep section.
2.3	Time for some downhill! The dirt road becomes whoopy, rocky, and narrower as you descend.
2.5	The trail becomes singletrack! (Unless ATVs have been using it). Keep heading straight on the trail; slightly veering right. Soon it becomes more of a speed racer course!

3.0	Cross Dry Creek, and go right on the dirt road. If the creek is full, there is usually a log crossing to the right. [Riding left takes you onto the Dry Creek Loop; see Ride 11, Mile .3].
3.3	Merge right on the dirt road. Soon, veer right again onto the main graded road. Just behind you is the trailhead to Inyo Craters Singletrack (Ride 12), another great addition to the ride.
3.6	Turn right and ride up the Scenic Loop Road (paved) for a short spurt.
3.8	Pedal left onto the dirt road (somewhat faint at first), which will veer right and parallel the paved road. Soon you will come to a super steep (but relatively short) hill climb. [A quicker and less challenging way to climb back is by staying on the paved Scenic Loop Road for the next 1.5 miles].
4.0	Disregard the offshoot road to the left and keep cranking straight on the main route. Up ahead there will be some bailout roads on the right leading to the paved road, although the pace gets easier.
4.6	As you reach the top of the climb and the road turns 90 degrees to the left, make a sharp righthand turn up a bank and onto another dirt road. Keep veering right ahead.
5.0	Ride through the large pullout off of road 3S24 by turning right and pedaling toward the Scenic Loop Road. Just before reaching the paved road, turn left onto the trail. The remainder of this ride is an out & back.
6.7	Back to the start. [To continue on the Downtown trail, ride to HWY 203 and cross over to the flat open area. After crossing Uptown trail, you'll come to the Downtown trail. Go left and cruise down].

Dry Creek Loop

Location: Off Mammoth Scenic Loop near the Inyo Craters.
Distance: 7 miles.
Elevation: 8090/8690 ft.
Trail Surface: 37% singletrack/mx trail; 63% narrow dirt road.
Type of Ride: Loop.
Terrain: Dry Creek; Lodgepole pine forest; pumice flat.
Technical Level: Medium/Difficult; some pumice and ruts.
Exertion Level: Moderate/Strenuous; with steady climbing.

A tree slalom down to Dry Creek.

Highlights: This forested loop parallels Dry Creek for much of the ride. After climbing some narrow dirt roads, the ride joins Mountain View Trail for a jaunt before descending some slithering singletrack. Along the way, it passes through a seismic feature much like the Earthquake Fault! Dry Creek Loop has the remote feeling of riding in a lonely forest and some of the stashes of singletrack might inject you with sensations of euphoria!

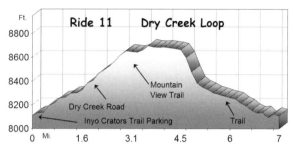

Options: For an excellent longer ride, add on Scenic Loop Trail Ride (Ride 10) and/or the Inyo Craters Singletrack (Ride 12). This ride also tangents the Mountain View Trail (Ride 3) making for some great figure eight loop possibilities as well.

Note: Watch out for speedy dirt bikers on the trails.

Bouncing off a whoopty-doo.

Directions/Access: From North Village area in Mammoth, drive up HWY 203 toward the ski area. Turn right on Mammoth Scenic Loop Road. Go 2.2 miles and turn left at the "Inyo Craters Sign" onto the graded dirt road (3S30). After about 1/3 mile, the road splits at the sign labeled "Inyo Craters;" veer right. Immediately, there will be dirt pull-out/parking area on the right. Park here. Or better yet, bike Ride 10 to the trailhead.

Mileage Guide	
0.0	From the dirt pull-out/Inyo Craters dirt road, take the dirt road that's perpendicularly heading away - opposite the parking area.
.30	On the left, you will pass an intersection that crosses the

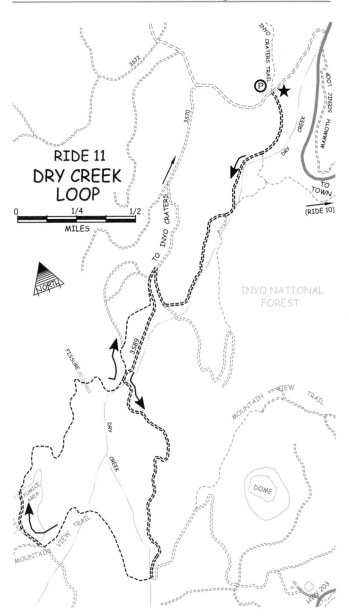

RIDE 11
DRY CREEK
LOOP

0   1/4   1/2
MILES

NORTH

3572

3570

3589

TO INVO CRATERS

INVO CRATERS TRAIL

DRY CREEK

MAMMOTH SCENIC LOOP

TO TOWN
(RIDE 10)

INYO NATIONAL
FOREST

FISSURE

DRY CREEK

PUMICE AREA

MOUNTAIN VIEW TRAIL

MOUNTAIN VIEW TRAIL

DOME

HWY 203

	creek which leads to the Scenic Loop Trail. Stay straight on the narrow dirt road that parallels Dry Creek.
.60	Pass a trail on the left as you encounter a quick steep section of road. This solitary road becomes progressively more trail-like with berms and whoopty-doos.
1.1	Grunt through the sandpit section. At the next intersection, turn right on the road.
1.3	Turn left at this intersection, onto 3S89/"Dry Creek Road." Stay on this road as you climb up toward the Mountain View Trail.
2.4	Periodic views of Mammoth Mountain help give a sense of direction.
2.9	Go right onto the singletrack labeled "Mountain View."
3.7	Pedal right on the dirt road. Soon you will come to an intersection of pumice roads; go straight (veering right). This pumice road splits and goes around both sides of this large pumice motorcycle play area. Veer left around the left-hand side of the open area to catch the main road through the flat. Head up the bank on the far side. This is a good place to take in the sights; all of Mammoth Mountain is behind and the San Joaquin Ridge is to the left.
3.9	After climbing up the pumice bank, most of the motorcycle tracks will converge forming a progressively more pronounced trail. After a slight uphill, this trail bears slightly right and down the backside. Eventually, the trail will become more compact and steeper with banked turns.
4.7	The trail passes over a seismic fissure here.
4.9	Merge with road! The trail tangents the road for a second before veering off again to the left.
5.1	Split! Make a sharp right.
5.4	Go left when you reach Dry Creek Road/3S89; the rest of the ride is an out & back.
5.5	At the intersection, turn right on the dirt road to continue

	back the way you came. [An excellent alternative for the rest of the ride is to keep heading straight down the road to the Inyo Craters Singletrack. At the Inyo Craters Road intersection, turn left and follow signs. The trail is behind the restrooms in the parking area. The Inyo Craters Singletrack takes you right back to the original trailhead. See Ride 12 for more detail].
5.7	Turn left onto the 4x4 road and continue on.
6.9	Go left and head back to the trailhead parking area.
7.0	All done.

Inyo Craters Singletrack

Inyo Craters Singletrack in the fall.

Location: Off the Mammoth Scenic Loop Road by the Inyo Craters.
Distance: 2.9 miles.
Elevation: 7980/8190 ft.

Trail Surface: 70% singletrack; 30% dirt road/path.
Type of Ride: Out & Back
Terrain: Rolling hills; pines & aspens; meadows; Deer Mountain views; volcanic explosion pits.
Technical Level: Easy.
Exertion Level: Moderate.

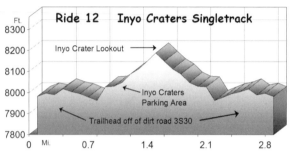

Highlights: This is some of the smoothest non-motorized singletrack in Mammoth! On its way to the Craters, the trail grooves and winds through an open pine forest with sneak peeks of the surrounding mountains from various meadows. At the Inyo Craters, you'll experience the striking evidence of

Riding in front of Deer Mountain, one of the Inyo Craters.

Mammoth's turbulent past. These explosion pits were formed just 600 years ago when the hot underground magma instigated a powerful blast in three spots. This eruption is to blame for the pumice-covered terrain of the surrounding area. You'll also note that small lakes have formed in the bottom of these 100 and 200-foot depressions. Deer Mountain, to the north, encloses the highest of the

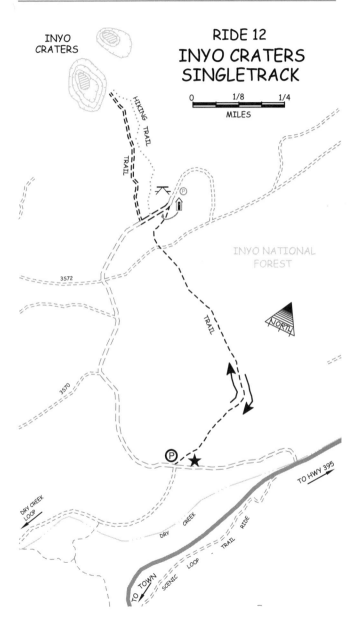

RIDE 12
INYO CRATERS
SINGLETRACK

INYO CRATERS

HIKING TRAIL

TRAIL

0   1/8   1/4
MILES

INYO NATIONAL
FOREST

3S72

TRAIL

NORTH

3S70

P

★

TO HWY 395

DRY CREEK LOOP

DRY CREEK

SCENIC LOOP   TRAIL RIDE

TO TOWN

Inyo Crater group. Don't miss the splendid backdrop of the San Joaquin Ridge and Mammoth Mountain!

Options: You can lock up your bike (or stash in the woods) and hike around the Inyo Craters area. To tackle more miles, ride the Dry Creek Loop (Ride 11) and/or the Scenic Loop Trail Ride (Ride 10).

Note: The Inyo Craters are a high-use tourist area and bikes are not allowed on the hiking trails around the craters.

Directions/Access: From North Village area in Mammoth, drive up HWY 203 toward the ski area. Turn right on Mammoth Scenic Loop Road. After about 2 ¾ miles, turn left at the "Inyo Craters Sign" onto the graded dirt road (3S30). After about 1/3 mile, the road splits at the sign labeled "Inyo Craters;" veer right. Immediately, there will be a dirt pull-out/parking area on the right. The trailhead starts here, at the brown mountain biking sign. If you are biking to the trail, take Uptown Trail (Ride 2) to the Scenic Loop Trail (Ride 10).

Mileage Guide	
0.0	At the parking area, take the trail at the brown bicycle sign.
.80	Cross the dirt road and continue by the trail. Better downshift, because this next section is steep!
.90	The main Inyo Craters parking area. Go left, past the restroom, on the graded dirt road.
1.0	On the right you'll see the official trailhead sign. (These are the hiking-only trails). Just beyond this, however, is an old road/path with a green pole in the middle. Ride up this.
1.1	Stay to the left.
1.4	The first of the Inyo Craters. You can lock up your bikes or hide them in the woods here and hike around the craters. When you're finished exploring, turn around and ride back the way you came.
1.7	Go left at the dirt road.

1.8	Turn left at the dirt road.
2.0	Cross the road and continue on the trail.
2.8	Trailhead.

Other Riding Nearby

A. Inyo Craters Loop

The Inyo Craters Loop is a USFS-designated ride on 9.6 miles of scenic dirt and pumice roads. Technically, its rather easy, with a moderate exertion level. There are plenty of biker signs labeling the route in both directions. The wide roads roam through giant pumice flats and into a large Jeffrey pine forest, through which Deadman Creek flows. Bikers are confronted with the San Joaquin Ridge, White Wing Mountain, and more distant peaks and ridges. To reach the trailhead, bike the Scenic Loop Trail Ride (Ride 10) or drive up HWY 203 toward the ski area. Turn right on Mammoth Scenic Loop Road. After about 2.7 miles, turn left at the "Inyo Craters Sign" onto the graded dirt road (3S30). After about 1/3 mile, the road splits at the

The Inyo Craters Loop crosses a large pumice flat
before entering a Jeffrey pine forest.

sign labeled "Inyo Craters;" veer right and follow signs to the Inyo Craters parking area.

B. Big and Little Smokey Loops

Big and Little Smokey Loops are also signed official USFS routes on fairly wide dirt and gravel roads. They are technically easy and moderately strenuous aerobically. The "trailhead" is about 4 miles north of the Mammoth Lakes turnoff on HWY 395. Just after passing Smokey Bear Flat, there is a gravel road heading to the right. Parking is in a pullout to the left of this road near the Mountain Bike sign.

Smokey says "only you can seize the day!"

Two loops commence from this sign. The Big Smokey Loop is 13.8 miles and has views ranging from Bald and Lookout Mountains and other eastern views, along with Sierra views. The ride contours the forested hills and open pumice flat areas. The Little Smokey Loop is a smaller version of the ride at 6.2 miles. Both routes are well signed at all major intersections.

Shady Rest Forest Loop

Turning the tires in a shady forest near town.

Location: Shady Rest Park, starting at Forest Trail Road.
Distance: 3.5 miles.
Elevation: 7770/7900 ft.
Trail Surface: 74% singletrack; 26% narrow dirt road.
Type of Ride: Loop with an Out & Back section.
Terrain: Jeffrey pine forest; town park; nearby campground.
Technical Level: Easy.
Exertion Level: Mild.

Highlights: Close to town, this easy ride is a short, mostly-singletrack loop through Jeffrey pine forest. While all levels of riders would probably enjoy cruising the Shady Rest forest, it is particularly suitable for families and beginner bikers. These smooth trails are often the first ridden as the spring snow starts to melt. Nearby, the Shady Rest Park has many facilities to be utilized.

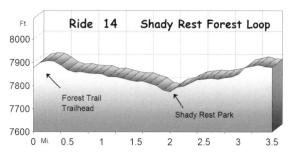

Options: Try riding the opposite direction. For a much longer ride, combine with the Mammoth Knolls Loop (Ride 15). The loop can be commenced from many locations; from the campground, the central Shady Rest parking area, or visitor center. You will also be passing near the Shady Freestyle zones (Ride 16A). For more play, check it out (see map below).

Note: You will pass by several dirt roads that criss-cross,

merge, and weave all over the place; sometimes creating a little confusion. Never fear! You have the guidebook! Also, usually you wont see anyone, but don't forget to be watchful when crossing any roads

It's never too hot near Shady Rest.

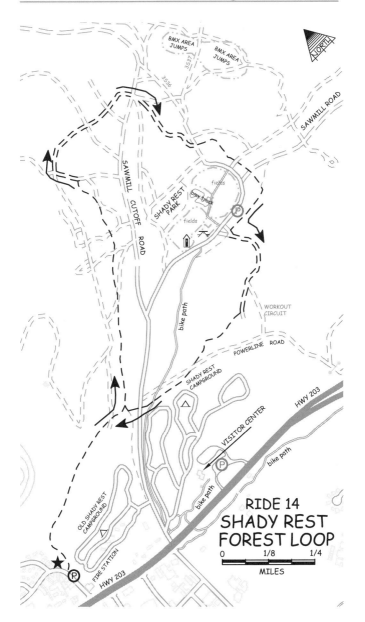

BMX AREA JUMPS

BMX AREA JUMPS

3537

NORTH

3536

SAWMILL ROAD

SAWMILL CUTOFF ROAD

SHADY REST PARK

fields

bmx track

fields

bike path

WORKOUT CIRCUIT

POWERLINE ROAD

SHADY REST CAMPGROUND

VISITOR CENTER

HWY 203

bike path

bike path

OLD SHADY REST CAMPGROUND

FIRE STATION

HWY 203

RIDE 14
SHADY REST
FOREST LOOP

0   1/8   1/4

MILES

just in case there are cars or motorcycles.

Directions/Access: Take Main Street/203 to Forest Trail Road near the Fire Station (a block west of the intersection of HWY 203 and Old Mammoth Road). Just beyond a "closed road" with a green gate, there is a little dirt parking area about 400 feet up Forest Trail road on the right. Look for the trail just past the telephone pole and a little biker symbol sign.

Mileage Guide	
0.0	From the trailhead parking area on Forest Trail Rd, take the trail leading into the forest veering left along a fence. As the fence ends, pass by the campground border path.
.50	Turn left when you reach a trail intersection area near Sawmill Cutoff Road, a paved road. This trail will roughly parallel the road for a while.
.90	Staying on the trail, cross the first of a series of dirt roads.
1.0	The trail briefly fuses with a dirt road here; keep left.
1.2	Merge left onto a dirt road. Soon you will come to another intersection; go right on the first road and keep riding straight through any other intersections.
1.5	Cross the main graded road. Just ahead on the right are two more dirt roads. Bypass the first road, which heads sharply right, and go straight on the perpendicular dirt road. Stay to the right when the road curves ahead, (ignoring the fainter roads on the left).
1.7	Turn right on the dirt road and pedal toward the fields. About 200 feet ahead, turn left on the singletrack.
1.9	The trail crosses a couple roads here.
2.0	Make a sharp right onto the trail.
2.2	Turn left on the dirt road, and ignore a road merging in from the left up ahead.
2.4	Split. Go right on the road, which soon becomes more of a trail. [Going left will take you to an interesting workout circuit/track].
2.5	Pedal right onto the singletrack trail.

2.7	Go right on the trail under the powerlines. When the trail splits ahead, go left.
2.9	After crossing the bike bath, pass over Sawmill Road (the paved road), and continue past the post to the left on the trail.
3.0	At the intersection, go straight on the trail, toward the powerlines (return the way you came).
3.5	Back at Forest Trail parking area.

Mammoth Knolls Loop

Location: Mammoth Visitor Center/Shady Rest Park area.
Distance: 12 miles.
Elevation: 7620/8480 ft.
Trail Surface: 16% singletrack; 35% narrow dirt road; 42% dirt road; 7% bike path.

Two singletracks for the price of one!

Type of Ride: Loop.
Terrain: Pine forest; vast mountain vistas; sagebrush; knolls.
Technical Level: Medium; occasional sand or rocks.
Exertion Level: Strenuous.

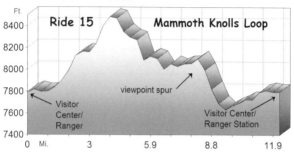

Highlights: This cross-country loop is just outside of town, yet it offers views of the entire region. In and out of the forest, the ride wanders among the knolls above the town of Mammoth Lakes. Your riding experience climaxes atop the Obsidian Knoll, with views ranging from the Glass and White Mountains through the length of the Sierras. Although it is mostly on dirt roads, the ride is one of the closest and more rewarding pedals around.

A small slice of the panorama from one of the knolls;
Mammoth Mountain and the Sierra Crest.

Options: There are some shorter possibilities. Sawmill Cut-off Road bisects the center of the ride and can easily be used to bike either half of the loop. See also "Other Riding Nearby" below. Additional miles come with the combination of the Scenic-Loop Trail Ride (Ride 10), which can be accessed by riding left on 3S33 at the intersection of Mile 4.2 in the Mileage Guide below.

Note: This ride is in a multi-use area, so be careful not to startle the motorcyclists and jeepsters.

Directions/Access: The ride starts at the bike path in front of the Visitors Center/Ranger Station in Mammoth Lakes. The Ranger Station is one of the first rights off HWY 203 as you are coming into town (a block before reaching Old Mammoth Road). Park in the main parking lot.

Mileage Guide	
0.0	Strike out on the bike path leading away from the Ranger Station/Visitor Center.
.10	Stay straight. (The bike path splits and goes under the bridge on the left).
.20	Just before the stop sign, go right at the bike path split. Soon, the bike path crosses the road. To ride singletrack, go left past the kiosk and though the intersection. Spot the trail on the right, next to the gray brick box. This trail will parallel Sawmill Cutoff Road and pass along the campground.
.50	Cross the paved road and continue on the trail. Ahead, you will come to a trail intersection; keep going straight. The trail will pass by some perpendicular dirt roads.
1.0	Keep on the trail as you pass the third dirt road.
1.2	The trail ends at the dirt road; go left.
1.3	As you come to a major intersection of dirt roads, ride left at the first dirt road. Stay on this dirt road for a few miles as you climb the first knoll. Ignore all the random roads that spur off to the sides.
1.7	At this split, go straight along the power lines.
1.8	Veer right at this next split, and pedal up the hill following the blue diamond symbols in the trees.
2.3	Disregard the road heading down on the right.

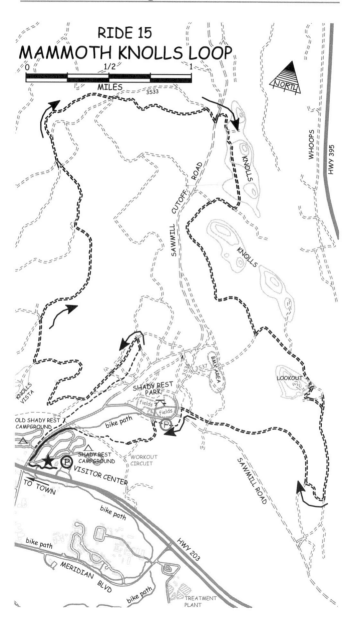

RIDE 15
MAMMOTH KNOLLS LOOP

0   1/2   1
MILES

NORTH

3533

KNOLLS

KNOLLS

WHOOPS

HWY 395

SAWMILL CUTOFF ROAD

LOOKOUT

KNOLLS
VISTA

3537 3537
BMX AREA

SHADY REST
PARK
fields   fields

OLD SHADY REST
CAMPGROUND

bike path

SAWMILL ROAD

SHADY REST
CAMPGROUND

WORKOUT
CIRCUIT

VISITOR CENTER

TO TOWN

bike path

HWY 203

bike path

bike path

MERIDIAN BLVD

bike path

TREATMENT
PLANT

2.7	Top of this section; head down the hill. [To the left is Knolls Vista, a somewhat worthwhile spur].
2.9	As you reach the bottom, stay on the main road, as two roads head left. Enjoy the easy riding now; soon you'll encounter the hardest climb of the ride.
3.5	It's getting pretty darn steep now. If it hasn't rained, its probably sandy. So point it and attack! Audible grunts may help here. If you need a breather, make sure you look behind at the refreshing summit-filled horizon.
3.7	At the right-hand curve in the road, ignore the road bearing off to the left.
4.2	Stay on the main road. You'll pass a road on the right and two roads on the left. [One of the roads on the left, 3S33, leads to the Scenic Loop Trail, about 2 miles farther down].
4.4	Look for an old 4x4 road heading down on the left. Take it!
5.0	Another 5-way intersection. Go straight across the road and up the little hill to a double track.
5.2	The road makes a major left turn here.
5.3	Now the road makes a 90 degree right turn downhill.
5.6	Merge right when you reach the major dirt road, and keep heading down.
5.7	Stay left and cross the main graded dirt road. Then take the road heading up a little to the left. As you head up ignore the spur roads off to the sides.
5.8	Pass by the road on the left, and any more offshoot roads ahead.
6.2	Downhill for a bit! At the next split in the road, roll right downhill.
6.5	Pedal left at this split. Soon some incredible mountain sights will appear.
7.6	Intersection. Crank left uphill.
7.9	Bike straight (right), dismissing the road on the left.

8.1	Top of this section. There is a short but steep road to the right that goes to a must-see-it viewpoint on the top of Obsidian Knoll. All the Eastern Sierra will be present at the top! Moving on, aim down the steep and rocky-at-first road.
8.3	Turn right onto the switchback road.
8.4	Stay left at the turn.
8.5	As you reemerge on the original road, it will be steep and rutted with little whoops.
9.0	Go right onto the road.
9.2	Intersection at power lines. Roll right.
10.0	Go straight past any spur roads to the left and right.
10.2	Ride left on the singletrack. Soon you will cross a road, stay on the singletrack.
10.3	At the split go right.
10.5	At the perpendicular road, pedal left up the road.
10.6	Split, stay to the right.
10.7	Soon you'll reach another split, veer right and the road will soon become more trail-like.
10.9	Bear right off the old roadbed and onto the singletrack.
11.1	Veer right under the power lines.
11.2	Splits. Ride left, passing trails that descend to the camp-sites.
11.3	At the bike path, go left.
11.6	Heed the stop sign and cross the road to continue on the bike path.
11.7	Left at junction.
11.9	Ends at visitor Center.

Other Riding Nearby

A. Shady Rest BMX & Freestyle Zones

Get Air! A small jump area for kids is tucked away near the bathrooms on the far side of the park. Another larger area has a mini track with various jumps and whoops. It can get sandy in the summer, especially if motorcycles are frequenting the area. From the farthest paved parking near the rear fields, it's ½ mile away. Take road 3S36 a short distance (near Mile 1.7 in the Ride 14 Mileage Guide above). Turn right on 3S37 and stay to the right as you climb up to the freestyle area. This originally was a BMX track area for kids, and might be boring for hardcore freeriders.

B. Knolls Trails

Follow your Knolls.

There are many other trails and roads to add variety to the Shady Rest Forest and Knolls Loop Rides. Some fun alternatives use the existing motorcycle trails that steeply drop off a couple of the knolls. One such 6-mile loop will add a little spice to the first part of the section of the Knolls loop. While retaining some of the scenic climbing, various segments of singletrack in the area are incorporated into the downhill sections. The trails are not for beginners; it is often steep and relatively sandy – but loads of fun!

Follow the Mammoth Knolls Loop (Ride 15), to Mile 2.7 on

the ride's Mileage Guide and pedal toward the Knolls Vista offshoot. Just ahead, take the trail veering off to the right, before the road gets really steep. A quick singletrack section of steep, banked turns takes you to a road across from the water tank. Go right on the road, which will merge left into the Knolls Loop in .5 miles. After a long steep climb, go left at the split in the roads. About .6 miles after descending, look for the singletrack descending on the left. Take it!

Keep veering right and you will eventually end up back at the water tank. After heading back to the main road, you can take any of the trails descending down the hillside toward Forest Trail Road. For starters, you may want to take the trail just to the right of the drainage. At Forest Trail Road, you can ride back to town, or to the start of the Shady Rest Forest Loop (Ride 10) toward the left.

C. Whoopty-Doos

Some of the many roads in the area are highly used by ATVs and motorcycles. These trails are sandy and extremely whooped out: some riders hate these conditions and avoid these trails at all costs. However after a lot of rain, the whoops can actually be fun! The downhill sections are rhythmic, while the slightest uphill takes considerable effort. The general area of these trails and roads is beyond the backside of the Shady Rest area. A graded dirt road that bisects the Knolls Loop, 3S08, leads toward this area. One main whooped-out route parallels HWY 395, passing volcanic areas with steam vents and sporadic mountain views, including Mt Morrison. There's a lot out there to explore!

A whooped-out motorcycle trail aimed at Mount Morrison.

Town Bike Paths

Riding to a lookout area with Mammoth Mountain behind.

The town of Mammoth Lakes has done a good job building bike paths around the town, making autos unnecessary in the summer months. Some of the bike paths parallel town roads and are convenient for getting to residential and business areas. Others are more remote with amazing views, and make family riding much easier. There are about 8 miles of paved bike paths, not including the sidewalks on Old Mammoth Road. The town has more planned in the near future. Best of all, these paths facilitate riding to various mountain biking trailheads from almost anywhere in town.

A popular section of the bike path system stretches from Mammoth Creek Park down to the bottom of Meridian Blvd. From there, it splits and heads back up to the high school one way, and up to the Ranger Station/Visitor Center the other way. There is also a fragmented section of trail that runs from Juniper Springs Lodge down to Snowcreek. Also, a path skirts part of Sierra Star Golf Course bisecting through the heart of town. Soon a path will also link up in Old Mammoth.

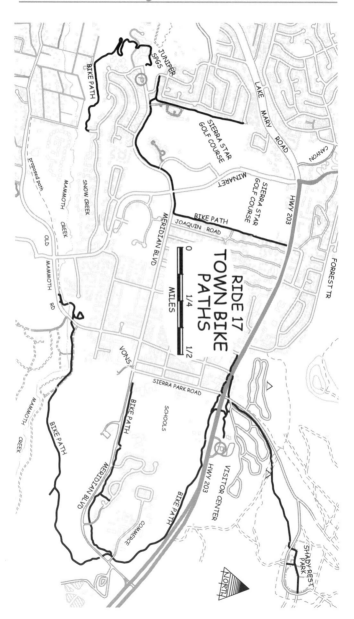

RIDE 17
TOWN BIKE
PATHS

Laurel Lakes Ride

Laurel Lakes 4x4 road.

Location: Just south of Mammoth off of Sherwin Creek Road.
Distance: 10.4 miles (5.2 each way).
Elevation: 7300/10,150 ft.
Trail Surface: 100% jeep road.
Type of Ride: Out & Back.

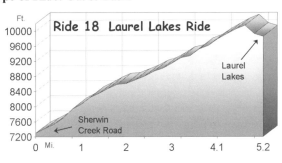

Terrain: High Sierra canyon; lakes; shale; aspen groves; meadows; hanging valleys; sagebrush; Laurel Creek.

Technical Level: Difficult; very rocky.

Exertion Level: Very Strenuous; the climb on this ride is a grunting leg burner!

Watch out for hungry ruts that might eat you alive!

Highlights: The Laurel Lakes jeep route is a gravelly road at best, and it gradually gets rockier and rougher. This is the type of road that excludes most vehicles except 4x4 high clearance trucks or jeeps. NORBA Downhill Racers have been known to practice on the rough terrain by doing shuttle rides, while superman climbers are challenged by the heart-wrenching uphills.

This wilderness-like ride commences in sagebrush and ends in a quintessential High Sierra alpine setting; a ridge and tree-framed lake. As you climb, Laurel and Bloody Mountains loom out in front of you. Lots of wildlife such as deer, coyotes, marmots, and native trout are all common in the vicinity. The aspen-lined creek makes riding in the Fall absolutely amazing! You also will notice the evidence of the area's past mining history in the old roads that steeply ascend the sheer mountain slopes to numerous mine shafts.

The rewarding-but-bumpy descent reveals blurred images of

The cow-greeters at the trailhead.

Crowley Lake, the White Mountains, Hot Creek, Glass Mountains, Antelope Valley, Mammoth Mountain, San Joaquin Ridge, and plenty of other amazing scenery!

Options: Talk your friends or family into 4x4'ing up to Laurel Lakes to hike, fly fish or hangout; so you can shuttle up and bike the downhill!

Note: This is a true multi-use trail; be courteous to horseman, 4X4's, hikers, and motorcycles.

Directions/Access: From Mammoth Lakes, take Old Mammoth Road through town and turn left on Sherwin Creek Road (across from Mammoth Creek Park). Drive or ride just over 4 miles to Laurel Lakes Road on the right. There is a dirt pullout for parking. If you are driving from south of Mammoth Lakes, take Sherwin Creek Road directly from HWY 395. The trailhead is 1 ½ miles ahead on the left.

A piece of what's waiting at the top: a section of upper Laurel Lake.

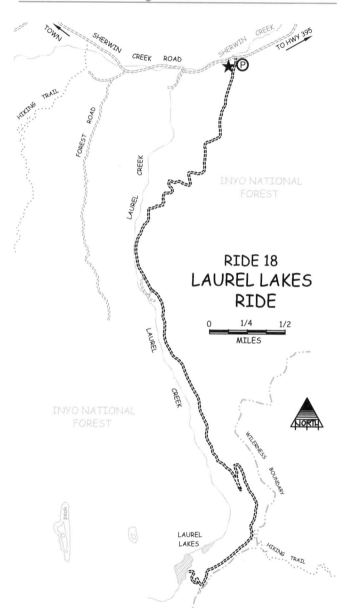

RIDE 18
LAUREL LAKES
RIDE

Mileage Guide	
.00	Set off on the gravelly road, which soon worsens.
2.2	On the right, a road descends into aspens surrounding the creek. This is a primo spot to take a break or camp, especially in the fall.
3.4	Another road on the right descends into the meadow area. Below the cascading creek, keep an eye out for deer and other wildlife.
4.5	A backpacker trail ascending on the left (no bikes) eventually drops into Convict canyon and connects with other backcountry hiking trails. As you continue on, you will soon see the first small lake below.
4.8	Highest point of the ride! On the right, the road switchbacks down to the upper lake.
5.2	Pullout area on the lake. After you've had your fill of peace and tranquility, bomb down the way you came up!

Deer on the Laurel Lakes Road.

South of Mammoth

Owens River Gorge Loop

Above the Owens River Gorge.

Location: South of Mammoth; off 395, opposite Tom's Place.

Distance: 7.6 miles (or 11.6 miles with 4 mile addition).

Elevation: 6690/7150 ft.

Trail Surface: 15% singletrack; 81% dirt road; 4% paved road.

Type of Ride: Loop.

Terrain: High desert meadows; chaparral; lush cottonwoods & aspens; Owens River and Gorge; Sierra views; Owens River Gorge; Jeffrey pines; boulder piles.

Technical Level: Medium; with a fairly difficult trail section.

Exertion Level: Moderate.

Highlights: The Owens River Gorge Loop is a wonderful way to get off the beaten track and into the sunny high desert. Most of the ride loops above the gorge on empty dirt roads and doubletrack. Facing the distant Ritter Range, a relatively unknown singletrack suddenly contours the steep banks of the gorge falling almost 400 feet in 1.1 miles. Since this trail was an old mining access route, it is a bit overgrown and can be treacherous with rockfall potential. At the same time, it is one of the highlights of the ride. For much of the year except for peak winter months, the loop makes a wonderfully warm and sunny way to get some fresh air excersize.

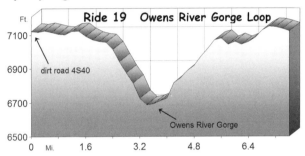

Options: A seemingly endless supply of roads crisscross and circle around this entire area providing for a plethora of options. Also, there is a convenient bike/pedestrian tunnel under HWY 395 which can connect this ride with the Sand Canyon ride area.

Vast expanses of high desert doubletrack.

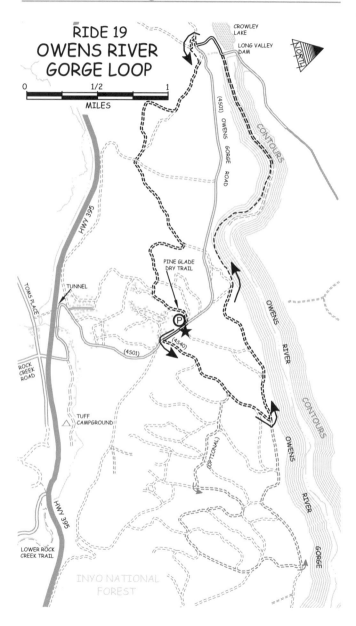

RIDE 19
OWENS RIVER
GORGE LOOP

CROWLEY LAKE

LONG VALLEY DAM

NORTH

0   1/2   1
MILES

(4S01) OWENS GORGE ROAD

HWY 395

CONTOURS

TUNNEL

PINE GLADE DRY TRAIL

TOMS PLACE

ROCK CREEK ROAD

P

(4S01)   (4S40)

OWENS RIVER

TUFF CAMPGROUND

OWENS RIVER

CONTOURS

(OPTIONAL)

HWY 395

LOWER ROCK CREEK TRAIL

OWENS RIVER GORGE

INYO NATIONAL FOREST

Note: Some sections of the roads are relatively sandy, depending on time of year and amount of OHV use.

Directions/Access: From Mammoth, take Highway 395 south about 14 miles and turn left on Owens Gorge Road (4S01).

Riding into the Owens River Gorge.

Follow the road about two and a half miles through a housing area and then past a couple dirt roads off to the right. After passing Pine Glade Road on the left, park in the pullout at Pine Glade Dry Trail. From Bishop, take 395 north and turn right on Owens Gorge Road. Then follow the above directions.

	Mileage Guide
0.0	From the pullout at Pine Glade Dry Trail, turn right and backtrack on the paved road.
.20	Turn left at the dirt road 4S40, just beyond the top of a little hill.
.50	At the split, pedal left.
.70	Pass the faint road veering off to the left.
.90	Stay straight (left) at this split. To ride a longer loop, however, go right.
1.1	Yet another fork; stay left (straight).
1.2	Go left on the road following the ridge above the gorge.
1.5	As you ride through the boulder pile area, ignore a series of 3 sandy roads heading off to the left.
2.3	Important intersection! This 4-way split is in the flat area before the road ascends again. The singletrack, which is not very obvious at first, is diagonally straight ahead to the right. The trail starts beyond the boulders at a small

	pullout. Enjoy the amazing views of the gorge and sur-rounding mountains, but be alert and careful as you descend the trail. As it traverses a steep cliff through somewhat overgrown ankle-biter bushes, there are occasional boulder blockages and the trail may be covered with rocks at anytime. Also, be very cautious of falling rocks in this steep terrain, which could potentially make this trail treacherous. Its paced at a relatively gentle grade…just don't take any big falls!
3.4	At the bottom, turn left at the road and follow along the river on your way back up. [You may first want to journey off to the right. The road ends shortly at some primitive hiking and fishing trails along the river. Scenery and wildlife abound].
3.6	Off to the right, you'll pass a bridge at a pretty fishing spot fenced with lush cottonwoods.
4.0	Climb left up the hill.
4.3	Keep riding. At the top you'll reach pavement by the dam.
4.5	At the curve in the road, take the bypass trail up the hill side just before the gated dirt road on the right. Then merge onto the road and crank on.
4.6	Follow the road to the left as it switchbacks around (passing a road leading to the lake).
4.7	On the curve, take the trail left.
4.8	The trail will merge in to the road. Soon you will merge right onto another road. Press on.
5.6	Keep riding straight, as a road comes in from the right.
5.9	At the 4-way split, pedal straight on through. Farther ahead, ride straight past two other spur roads.
6.6	At the fork in front of the large boulders, bike right.
7.1	Go right again at some smaller boulder piles. Soon there will be another intersection; go left (straight) and pass by a house.
7.4	Stay left on a graded dirt road.

| 7.6 | Return to original pullout. |

Sand Canyon Ride

Location: South of Mammoth Lakes; by Rock Creek Lake.
Distance: 12.6 miles; 24.5 mile loop with road.
Elevation: 6200/10200 ft.
Trail Surface: 17% singletrack; 81% dirt road; 2% paved road.
Type of Ride: One-Way Shuttle or Loop.
Terrain: Rock Creek Lake; creeks; pine & aspen forests; mountain ridge; panoramic views; meadows; high desert chaparral; granite outcroppings; steep sandy canyon.

A section of superb singletrack above Sand Canyon.

Technical Level: Difficult; some very rocky areas, one hike 'n' bike section, and some very steep, fast, and sandy sections.
Exertion Level: Moderate shuttle; Very Strenuous with loop.

Roaring down into Sand Canyon.

Highlights: Rating high on the fun meter, the Sand Canyon Ride drops 4,000 feet with ever-changing panoramic views that will make your eyes pop with delight. The ride contains some of the highest sections of bike-authorized singletrack in the Sierras, although most of the ride is on jeep roads. Commencing with a tough bike push section at the beginning, the riding is never boring and always variable: sometimes smooth doubletrack, then a boulder strewn rocky road, sandy fast bomber sections, a mega technical climb, and creek crossings. While some bikers prefer to shuttle the ride, the heart banging loop is a rite of passage for many local bikers and the earn-your-turns riders.

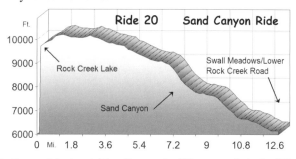

Options: Most notable of several offshoot roads is the Wheeler Crest jeep road at mile 4.1. See "Other Trails Nearby" below.

Loop: Cardiovores can ride 4,000 feet up the 9-mile Rock Creek Road to the trailhead. At the bottom, near Swall Meadows, ride 4 miles back up Lower Rock Creek Road to finish the loop. The lower section of the loop can also be done on

The trailhead is near Rock Creek Lake.

all dirt, making the last 4 ½ miles more of a real mountain bike ride. These last miles, however, include a very tough climb out of the valley. About 2 miles of the incline is on a sandy road, which can be very difficult to ride depending on the time of year. Walking the bike through long sandy uphills in late summer is not unheard of. For details on this option, refer to the map, the Directions/Access below, and Mile 10.8 on this Mileage Guide.

Lower Rock Creek Addition: Make a trip of epic proportions by combining Sand Canyon with Lower Rock Creek Trail (Ride 22). Although there's some climbing, it drops 5,300 feet over 22.6 miles! At the end of the Sand Canyon Ride, ride up the paved Lower Rock Creek Road (about 4 miles of uphill) to the trailhead and strike out on some of the best singletrack in the Sierra. For those who eagerly avoid pavement, the ride

Cooling off!

back up to the trailhead can also be done on dirt roads as discussed above in the Loop option.

Note: This ride, and all the associated options, can easily be turned into an all-day adventure. Be prepared with bike supplies and plenty of food and water!

Directions/Access:

Sand Canyon Shuttle Ride: To drop a vehicle off at the bottom of the ride, take HWY 395 south from Mammoth (or north from Bishop) to Lower Rock Creek Road. Drive 4 miles south to the junction with Swall Meadows Road and park.

A scenic meadow on a flatter part of the ride.

To reach the trailhead, drive back to HWY 395 and go north one exit to Rock Creek/Tom's Place. Drive up Rock Creek Road about 8.5 miles. You will pass Rock Creek Lake Lodge and come to an intersection. Go left here; there is a sign labeled "Rock Creek Lake Campground." This will take you around the backside of Rock Creek Lake. In less than ½ mile, there will be a parking lot on the right. Park here. The trailhead is approximately .2 miles farther up the road at a green gate on the left (across from the campground park host).

Sand Canyon Loop Ride: Park near the intersection of Crowley Lake Drive and Rock Creek Road near Tom's Place. Proceed to bike up Rock Creek Road for about 9.2 miles to the trailhead.

Shuttle with Lower Rock Creek Trail Addition: Park the lower shuttle vehicle at Paradise (see Directions/Access on Ride 22). To drive to the upper trailhead at Rock Creek Lake, follow the directions above.

Some singletrack near the top.

Mileage Guide

0.0	[If you ride up Rock Creek Road for the loop, add 9 miles to this Mileage Guide.] From the trail parking area at the lake, ride up Rock Creek Road and turn left at the "closed road" with a green gate. This is across from the campground host and dirt road. It is flat at first, but soon becomes steeper and rocky. You'll pass by campsites and then a cabin.
.20	After passing a group of 3 cabins, there will be a split in a rocky road. Go left. Soon, you'll arrive at a perpendicular road/trail. Go left again.
.50	A trail will merge in from the left. Keep heading straight up a very rocky trail.
.70	Don't be surprised to find yourself hiking this section; it is very difficult and steep. As you drag your bike up, don't miss the mountainous spectacle behind you!
1.3	At the split, bike left (straight). A wood sign labels the "Sand Canyon Mountain Bike Trail." The sandy-at-first trail quickly becomes an excellent singletrack!
1.6	Pass any trails veering off to the left and enjoy the descending singletrack as the vast mountain views open up to the south.
2.1	Creek Crossing!
2.3	Merge left onto the dirt road.
2.6	Here you'll encounter some uphill sections. Check out the northeastern vistas!
4.1	In this grassy area, an old mining road heads up Wheeler Ridge to the right. Pioneer-type riders may want to explore. More info is below at "Other Trails Nearby."
4.4	The ride gradually turns steeper here! Charge it!
7.0	Ignore any roads veering off in the area. The ride soon precipitously bombs its way down Sand Canyon!!!
8.4	After crossing a small creek, you'll soon notice the direct result of illegal campfires. The ride climbs uphill for a bit now.

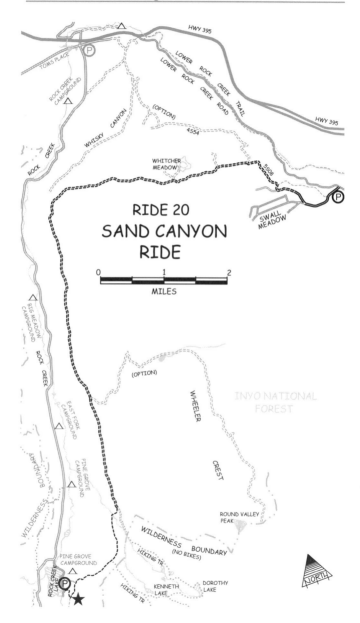

HWY 395

TOMS PLACE

LOWER ROCK CREEK

LOWER ROCK CREEK ROAD

LOWER ROCK CREEK TRAIL

HWY 395

ROCK CREEK CAMPGROUND

WHISKY CANYON

(OPTION)

4S54

5S08

ROCK CREEK

WHITCHER MEADOW

SWALL MEADOW

RIDE 20
SAND CANYON
RIDE

0   1   2
MILES

BIG MEADOW CAMPGROUND

ROCK CREEK

(OPTION)

WHEELER

INYO NATIONAL FOREST

EAST FORK CAMPGROUND

CREST

PINE GROVE CAMPGROUND

BOUNDARY

WILDERNESS

ROUND VALLEY PEAK

WILDERNESS BOUNDARY (NO BIKES)

PINE GROVE CAMPGROUND

ROCK CREEK LAKE

HIKING TR

HIKING TR

KENNETH LAKE

DOROTHY LAKE

NORTH

9.4	Major intersection at Witcher Meadow area! Stay on the main road; at a right curve, pedal right and head down the steep road toward a creek.
10.8	Split! Ride right toward Swall Meadows on 5S08. [If you want to loop back to Rock Creek Road on all dirt, go left on 4S54 under the power lines. This road becomes sandier and can turn into a nasty climb in the hot beating sun]. Biking to Swall Meadows will reveal visions of Lower Rock Creek Canyon, Owens Valley and the White Mountains.
11.6	Turn left on a graded dirt road, "Sky Meadow Ranch."
12.1	Go left onto the main paved road and ride down to the junction with Lower Rock Creek Road.
12.6	If you are shuttling, you should be back to the car. You can also ride the 4 miles up Lower Rock Creek Road to Ride 22 or farther on to the Crowley Lake Dr/Rock Creek Road intersection for the loop riders.

Optional Section continued from Mile 10.8 above:

The following is the alternative to riding up the paved Lower Rock Creek Road back to Tom's Place/Rock Creek Road, or Lower Rock Creek Trailhead. While there is not quite as much elevation to climb, this section is somewhat more demanding because of the loose soil. At least one mile of the road can get too sandy to ride.

10.8	At the split, go left on 4S54 under the power lines.
11.0	After crossing a small creek, prepare for a long climb.
13.0	Ignore the road on the left.
13.4	Finally! Some downhill relief!
13.7	Pass a another road on the left.
13.9	At the split, stay right. Ahead, you will veer right again.
14.3	Keep riding on the main dirt road. [Optional: To go to the Lower Rock Creek Trailhead, turn right onto the dirt road heading down toward the freeway before the road curves left toward Toms Place. When the road starts to curve back to the right, go straight (veering left) onto a very sandy semi-trail which leads toward the freeway

	through some dead bushes. At the freeway, go right along a faint sandy trail that parallels the freeway for a short distance. At the top of Lower Rock Creek Road, head down to the trailhead on the left. Please see Ride 22 for the details of the ride].
14.8	Go left on the paved road.
15.2	Ride ends at intersection near Tom's Place.

Gorgeous views are encountered in every direction.

Other Riding Nearby

A. Wheeler Crest

For one of the most climactic bikable routes in the Sierras, try riding the Wheeler Crest 4x4 road. It veers off the Sand Canyon Ride, at Mile 4.1 in the Mileage Guide above. Near a large alpine meadow at 9700 feet, the road steeply spirals up through forest. In 2 miles you actually descend to a lake, where the road will start to traverse the Wheeler Crest. As it passes some old mining prospects the views opening up will cause most bikers to succumb to gaping mouth syndrome.

Looking south at the end of the Wheeler Crest 4x4 road.

About 6 miles later, the road finally ends at the wilderness boundary at 11,200 feet, at the prospect below Round Valley Peak. This ride is not for the faint of heart. Besides being an incredible cardio work out, bikers are essentially above a 7,000 foot cliff - the equivalent of being in an airplane!

B. Swall Canyon Trail

This .9 mile trail is worth mentioning as a possible singletrack alternative to the last mile of the Sand Canyon shuttle ride. Much of it is sandy as it cruises down a small scenic canyon to Swall Meadow Road, above its junction with Lower Rock Creek Road. The inconspicuous trailhead is on the left just before reaching Sky Meadow Ranch Road and a small motor-cycle track/borrow pit, at Mile 11.6 in the Mileage Guide above. Since it parallels Lower Rock Creek Road, this trail is often noticed by bikers riding up the road from the Lower Rock Creek Loop.

Lower Rock Creek Trail

The one and only...Lower Rock Creek Trail!

Location: About 16 miles south of Mammoth Lakes off 395.

Distance: 8.1 miles one-way; 16 mile loop.

Elevation: 6880/4940 ft.

Trail Surface: 100% singletrack.

Type of Ride: One-Way Shuttle, or Loop.

Terrain: Pristine creek; mountain views; aspen groves; willows; huge Jeffrey Pines; boulders; high desert scenery.

Technical Level: Medium (first 2 sections); Very Difficult (last section); although recent trail work has mellowed it out a bit.

Exertion Level: Moderate with shuttle; Very Strenuous loop.

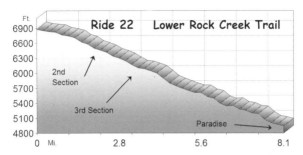

Highlights: Lower Rock Creek is the King Kong of all trails in the Eastern Sierra! This must-do ride will thrill you to goosebumps with flowing banked singletrack, fast slaloms through tunnels of aspen, and rocky technical sections. Dropping almost 2,000 feet, the trail passes in and out of lush riparian zones with wildflowers and thick vegetation. As it parallels the beautiful Lower Rock Creek, the canyon walls above are made up of Bishop Tuff and ancient volcanic ash. Keep your eyes open for basalt columns similar to Devil's Postpile on the canyon walls of the third section. The trail crosses Lower Rock Creek twice: the lower of the three sections is steeper, rockier, and much more technical than the top two. Riding the loop involves pedaling up the sunny and hot

That is a trail, and it is ridable!

Lower Rock Creek Road. Riding back up the trail is not recommended due to the amount of bikers flying down.

Options: Bikers can loop the top two sections for an easier 6.3 mile loop. For a much longer ride of epic proportions, combine with Sand Canyon Ride (Ride 20).

Note: Watch out for hikers, fisherman, and dog walkers!

A fast and furious descent.

Directions/Access: Drive about 16 miles south on HWY 395 from Mammoth Lakes. After passing the exit to Rock Creek Lake/Tom's Place, begin looking for the sign for Lower Rock Creek Road on the right. The trailhead dirt parking area is about 400 feet down Lower Rock Creek Road on the right. Alternative parking at the second and third sections are in dirt pullouts 2 miles and 3 miles farther down the road.

To drop a shuttle car at the bottom, continue driving about 8 miles down to Paradise Lodge.

From Bishop, you may not want to drive to the top. Take 395 North to the Rovana/Paradise turnoff, 9 miles. Make the first

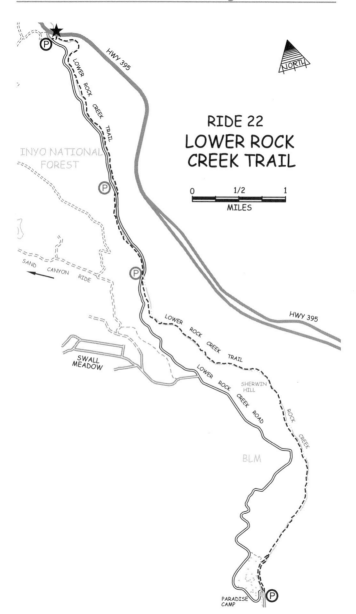

HWY 395

INYO NATIONAL FOREST

LOWER ROCK CREEK TRAIL

NORTH

RIDE 22
LOWER ROCK
CREEK TRAIL

0   1/2   1
MILES

SAND CANYON RIDE

LOWER ROCK CREEK TRAIL

HWY 395

SWALL MEADOW

LOWER ROCK CREEK ROAD

SHERWIN HILL

ROCK CREEK

BLM

PARADISE CAMP

right and drive about 5 miles to Paradise Lodge. The trailhead is just behind.

Gliding through the aspen groves.

Mileage Guide	
0.0	The upper trailhead is across from the dirt parking area.
2.2	As you come to Lower Rock Creek Road, turn right and ride back over the bridge. Go left, back onto the trail at the arrow sign.
3.3	Ride through the dirt parking area and go left through a gap in the railing on the other side of the road.
7.8	The trail widens here. (Up the hillside to the right is an alternative shortcut-trail that leads back to Lower Rock Creek Road).
7.9	Stay to the right and take the singletrack over the bridge.
8.1	The Paradise Restaurant is on the right. If you shuttled, the ride is over. If you are riding back up to the trailhead, turn right and follow Lower Rock Creek Road all the way back up.

Deep Canyon Singletrack Loop
(Tungsten Hills)

*The spectacular scenery of the Buttermilk Country frames
some amazing sections of singletrack.*

Location: West of Bishop, below the Buttermilk Country.
Distance: 9 miles.
Elevation: 6070/4900 ft.
Trail Surface: 40% singletrack; 46% dirt road; 14% graded road.
Type of Ride: Loop.
Terrain: Tungsten Hills & Buttermilk Country; mines; high desert rabbit & sage brush; Sierra peaks; glacier views; sun, sun, sun; panoramic views.

Technical Level: Medium/Difficult; some steeper sections with loose soil.

Exertion Level: Strenuous; a couple steep climbs.

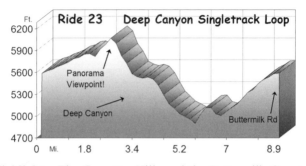

Highlights: The Tungsten Hills and the Buttermilk Country are a high desert area of boulders, creeks and meadows. These mine-studded foothills of the nearly 14,000 foot Mount Tom and Mount Humphreys, contain a mother lode of fun trails! This ride loops around McGee Creek and descends a single-track which roughly follows Deep Creek Canyon in the Tungsten Hills. The loop is filled with both challenging climbs and sweet amazing singletrack descents overlooking the greater Bishop area. After cruising through a meadow, the ride climbs to an astounding panorama hilltop. Then a perma-grin type of descent ensues followed by a climb over a boulder-strewn pass, and ends with a gradual climb back on a jeep road. Even though this is a

Flashbacks from an Eastern Sierra dream.

true multi-use area, filled with bikers, rock climbers, hikers, horseback riders, and various OHV users, you may not see anybody out there! This ride is an "offseason" ride, and is best ridden in the early spring and fall due to the heat. The trails are also at their best after recent rain or snowmelt.

Options: There are simply too many roads scattered about the Tungsten Hills and Buttermilk Country to mention. There's also quite a bit more motorcycle singletrack in the area, but some of it gets quite sandy.

Note: It gets hot out here; bring lots of water!

Riding through Longley Meadow toward Mount Tom.

Directions/Access: From Mammoth, go south on HWY 395 for 34 miles and turn right on Ed Powers Road. Drive 2.5 miles until you reach 168 and turn right. After about 2.5 miles Turn right again on Buttermilk Country Road/7S01.

In Bishop, drive west on Line Street/HWY 168 for almost 8 miles to Buttermilk Country Road/7S01, a graded dirt road.

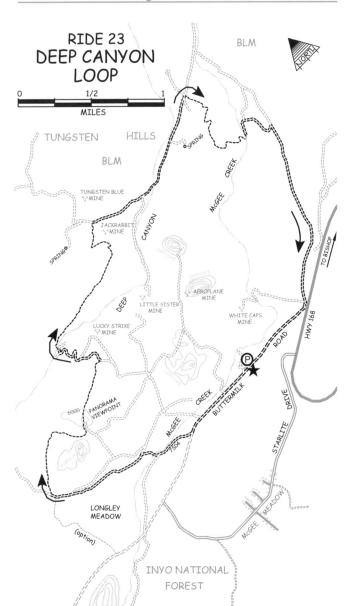

RIDE 23
DEEP CANYON
LOOP

0   1/2   1
MILES

TUNGSTEN   HILLS
BLM

BLM

SPRING

TUNGSTEN BLUE
MINE

JACKRABBIT
MINE

SPRING

DEEP
CANYON

McGEE CREEK

TO BISHOP

AEROPLANE
MINE

LITTLE SISTER
MINE

WHITE CAPS
MINE

LUCKY STRIKE
MINE

HWY 168

BUTTERMILK   ROAD

P

PANORAMA
VIEWPOINT

6000

McGEE CREEK

7504

STARLITE   DRIVE

LONGLEY
MEADOW

McGEE MEADOW

(option)

INYO NATIONAL
FOREST

NORTH

The trailhead is located just over half a mile down Buttermilk Road at a dirt road on the right. There is a pullout area for parking.

Mileage Guide	
0.0	From the parking/camping area, backtrack to Buttermilk Road and go right.
.60	Turn right onto the signed dirt road 7S04, just after Buttermilk Road curves left toward the Sierras and glacial views. You'll now be pedaling into Longley Meadow toward Mount Tom.
.90	Veer right and cross McGee Creek; a foot bridge is to the left of the road.
1.0	Stay on the main road to the left.
1.7	A superb singletrack spur option is on the left. It weaves its way through Longley Meadow and comes out at another road in a quarter mile. To stay on the main loop, however, keep pedaling straight for about 50 yards, and then turn right onto a road which immediately turns into singletrack. Farther up it will be signed "No ATVs."
2.1	After a curvy singletrack section, the trail will start to climb steeply. This is a will-testing brutal ascent; the most difficult of the ride. But, the reward is the empowering panoramic 360 degree lookout.
2.4	Just ahead, the trail will merge left onto the road that finishes the grueling climb to the top of the hill.
2.5	Panorama Viewpoint! From the rocky domed top of the hill, the views of Owen's Valley seem without end! To the west the boulders of the Buttermilks are framed by the glaciated Sierra peaks, with Mount Tom the closest. Looking over the mine studded Tungsten Hills, northern views range from the Wheeler Crest to Round valley and the Owen's River Gorge, and even beyond to Glass Mountains. Behind Bishop, the White Mountains look as dramatic as ever! After soaking in the enormity of the region, a fast whooped-out descent awaits!

3.0	After the 350-foot rollercoaster drop, ride left on the dirt road. Stay on this main route as it curves left and then down a hill. (Some roads will veer off to the right).
3.2	To continue on, stay left on the road as it heads down into valley with a (usually) dry creekbed. [If you like to explore, the Lucky Strike Mine is nearby on the road leading straight downhill to the right].
3.4	As you drop down into the valley known as Deep Canyon, you'll pass a wrecked cabin and trailer off in the bushes. Start looking on the left for the trail leading down into the trees, and cross over the creekbed. Resume on the trail on the other side.
3.6	The trail will start to descend again, passing another mine to the left.
4.2	Don't let the quicksand swallow you whole!
4.5	Merge left, down onto the jeep road.
4.6	Turn right onto the dirt road that descends further into Deep Canyon.
5.7	After passing a few roads on the right, look for the trail signed "no ATVs" on the right. This is opposite a road to the left. The singletrack is quite sandy at first, and may involve some hike-n-biking at the start.
6.2	Now for a dancing descent through the boulder garden!
6.5	The trail splits: to the right it is a very steep chute down to a bridge over the creek. Bike left to make your way around the steep pitch.
6.6	Cross the creek, and then merge straight onto the road up ahead.
6.7	Bear right at the split and start the climb back.
7.0	Merge right onto the road and stay to the right up the rockier road, which is not as sandy.
7.5	Keep pedaling straight on up.
8.3	At Buttermilk Road/7S01, turn right and ride back to your car.

| 8.9 | End of this loop. |

The joy of sweet singletrack!

Coyote Flat Ride

Bikepacking in the High Sierra.

Location: High in the Sierras west of Bishop and Big Pine.

Distance: 25.6 miles.

Elevation: 7,860/11,000 ft.

Trail Surface: 22% singletrack; 78% dirt road/doubletrack.

Type of Ride: One-way shuttle ride.

Terrain: High desert; meadows; forested areas; creeks; mega views in all directions of the Sierras, the White Mountains, and Owens Valley; glaciers; coyotes!

Technical Level: Medium/Difficult.

Exertion Level: Very strenuous; lots of tough climbing.

Highlights: Coyote Flat is a shuttle ride of truly myth making potential. Inevitable pain and hardship will be rewarded by the joys of accomplishment and the experience of riding high in the remote Sierras! Much of the ride is on jeep roads which sail in and out of meadows, along mountain ridges, through forest and high desert: all with everchanging views of the Sierras, White Mountains, and Owen's Valley. Because it is so remote and at such a high elevation, this ride is not for inexperienced riders or people who get lost easily. This ride climbs 3000 feet near Bishop and traverses the Sierras into the Baker Creek drainage 9 miles above Big Pine. The last 6 miles include some steep rocky singletrack. An alternate version of this ride cuts back to Bishop before the halfway point, making shuttling much quicker. In all aspects, this is one of the most demanding rides featured in this book.

The vicinity of the ride is included in the California Wilderness Bill, which threatens to close this entire area to most recreation uses except for hiking and pack horses. Time (and Congress) will tell the fate of the Coyote Flat Ride.

Crossing Coyote Creek.

Options: This ride can be turned into a full bikepacking trip. Along with many spur roads, there are some great campsites and tons of hiking potential!

Coyote Flat Alternatives: At 11 miles on the Mileage Guide of the traditional Coyote Flat Ride, there is a split at Coyote Creek that returns to Bishop. While the original ride requires

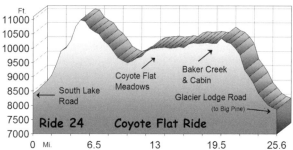

several more miles of scenic climbing and flat riding with a steep descent on technical singletrack, some people may prefer to have a much longer downhill with a shorter shuttle. This alternative section is on a 4X4-only road with fast banked turns that drops through 5,000 feet of pinyon pines and incredible rock formations! See "Continuation to Bishop Alternative" below the Mileage Guide for more details.

Another old road, which is used most often by motorcycles, departs the main route at Coyote Flat, and heads between Round and Sugarloaf Mountains before dropping down to Big Pine. This also has a much longer downhill on dirt than the traditional ride. At Mile 15 in the Mileage Guide below, you can take the split left. Bush crashing is likely in one area where this doubletrack is overgrown. Take a topographic map along for this adventurous option!

Coyote Flat framed by amazing Sierra peaks.

Note: This ride is extremely remote, take all supplies and be prepared for anything. This is a long shuttle and requires an early start. Some of the fainter trails are hard to find, and there are random roads veering off in all directions. Ride this only if you are both in supreme cardiovascular shape and self reliant in the outdoors. Taking a topo map is highly recommended.

Directions/Access:

To car drop in Big Pine: Take 395 south to Big Pine (about 55 miles south of Mammoth). Turn right on W. Crocker Ave, which will eventually turn into Glacier Lodge Road. Instead of driving to the end of the trail near the top, you may leave your car off the road at the bottom of the long incline.

To trailhead: Return to Bishop and go left (heading north) on West Line Street (168) at the light. After about 13 miles, turn left onto South Lake Road and drive for another 6 miles. One option for parking is in a turnout beyond Bishop Creek Lodge and the Mountain Lodge Store. The trailhead is actually .2 miles farther up South Lake Road, and left on the dirt road that looks like a driveway. Although it is labeled "Miller 2325," this is actually Forest Service land and the road/trail is a public easement. You may park in the small dirt pullout about 500 feet up this dirt road on the right.

To Alternative end point near Bishop: Take 395 to Bishop and go right on West Line Street (168) at the light. Then go left at Reata Road, which will lead into Coyote Valley Road. Park anywhere near the base of the incline.

Mileage Guide	
0.0	From the small dirt pullout, ride up the main dirt road. Ahead, take the bridge over the creek (there may be a chain gate you must pass over). Veer left when you pass by a large gray home. The road becomes doubletrack (if there is a large pile of dirt in the road; ride around it). It seems like you are on private property, but this is a Forest Service easement.
.20	Now you'll be riding up somewhat soft singletrack surrounded by sagebrush, as you climb up above a small community. This high desert's broad views are ever growing as you climb out of the valley.

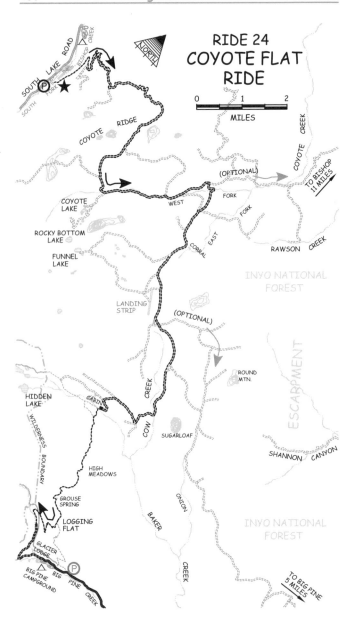

RIDE 24
COYOTE FLAT
RIDE

NORTH

0   1   2
MILES

SOUTH LAKE ROAD

BISHOP CREEK

SOUTH FORK

COYOTE RIDGE

COYOTE LAKE

ROCKY BOTTOM LAKE

FUNNEL LAKE

WEST FORK

(OPTIONAL)

COYOTE CREEK

TO BISHOP 11 MILES

EAST FORK

CORRAL

RAWSON CREEK

INYO NATIONAL FOREST

LANDING STRIP

(OPTIONAL)

ROUND MTN.

COW CREEK

HIDDEN LAKE

CABIN

WILDERNESS BOUNDARY

HIGH MEADOWS

SUGARLOAF

ESCARPMENT

SHANNON CANYON

GROUSE SPRING

LOGGING FLAT

GLACIER LODGE

BIG PINE CAMPGROUND

BIG PINE CREEK

ONION

BAKER CREEK

INYO NATIONAL FOREST

TO BIG PINE 5 MILES

1.3	As you reach the top of the moraine (a large glacial deposit), the trail will turn to doubletrack.
3.4	At the split, ride left through the granite outcroppings.
4.1	After a relieving descent into the woods, you'll spot a cabin on the right. The road becomes a little rockier and rougher as you continue to climb.
5.8	Yes! You are on top of the world! The vast amount of terrain below should divert your attention from those lactic acid-filled legs. Looking to the west and north will reveal an eagle's view of much of the High Sierras. To the east, the massive Owens Gorge and the ancient Bishop Tuff, which flowed out of the Long Valley caldera long ago, are all framed by the mighty White Mountains. Press on, and there will be more great views.
7.9	Ride straight. The road to the right heads up an alternate Coyote Ridge area and leads to several mines and meadow areas with western views of mountains and lakes, but eventually dead ends.
8.3	Stay left as you pass the Coyote Dry Lake turnoff to the right. [This area, however, is an ideal place to camp or explore if you have the time and energy. It is less than a mile to a grassy meadow, a dry lakebed, and a mine. A couple roads split off in the area, climbing to other mines and pretty views of a lake and mountains]. Continuing on with the ride, you will descend into an ever-lusher valley, cross Coyote Creek, and pass more mines.
11.0	Split! After riding through a valley and up a little hill, pedal right at the split for the full Coyote Flat ride. You soon will head down and cross the creek again. As you ride, ignore any faint roads/doubletracks that split off of the main dirt road. [For the alternative version of this ride that returns to Bishop, turn left at the split and skip to "Continuation to Bishop Alternative" below].
12.4	Go straight on the road here, passing the road heading toward the hillside on the right.

12.8	Again, go straight past a road that heads down to a corral on the left. Welcome to Coyote Flat!
13.4	Veer left and down on the road at this split.
14.2	Pedaling by the road which heads to Funnel Lake, ride straight and up a little hill.
15.0	After passing the Coyote Flat airstrip off to the right, a road will veer left up a drainage. This route, more often used by motorcyclists, eventually drops down to Big Pine. Pedal straight past this turnoff to continue on the main ride.
18.1	After crossing Cow Creek, you'll come to a large circular junction. Go right and climb up the road.
18.9	At the split, go left downhill. Enjoy the 14,000-foot mountainous vista surrounding the Palisade Glacier, the southernmost glacier in North America, and views of Big Pine far below.
19.2	Ride left at another split.
19.6	At this pretty spot, you'll come to Baker Cabin, located on aptly-named Baker Creek. Beyond this point, the ride turns mostly to singletrack. The trail is relatively unused, and it's a bit fainter and harder to follow at first. Pedal beyond the cabin between the horse rails, and follow a faint horse trail upstream. Ride along the barbed wire fence on the north side of the creek, and cross the creek about 50 feet upstream of where the fence spans across the creek. Once on the other side, there is a horse trail that comes from upstream along the creek and then curves perpendicularly uphill from the stream. Follow this narrow, and somewhat soft, trail uphill (to the south). See map for a depiction of this intersection.
19.9	At the fork, stay to the left and climb a bit more.
20.8	After dropping to a drainage near High Meadow, the trail ascends for one last big push!
21.4	This spectacular ridge is bounded by awe-inspiring sights from the Palisade Crest to the Big Pine Canyons.

	Above the Palisade glacier, Disappointment Peak, the Middle and North Palisade Peaks, and Mount Sills dominate the skyline. Get ready for a steep technical descent into the canyon!
22.0	The trail eases for a bit as you pass Grouse Spring and make your way toward the Logging Flat.
22.8	In the 1880's, Jeffrey pines were taken at the Logging Flat nearby. Note that a faint trail veers left and drops to Glacier Lodge Road here. Stay right with your hands on the brakes through the following steep switchbacks! Farther down, a short climb will interrupt the descent.
23.6	Intersection! Keep heading straight downhill. Soon the trail will turn and descend Big Pine Creek. Ahead, it will widen into an old dirt road.
24.4	Cross the creek near First Falls and pedal down the road.
25.0	Make a sharp left here and ignore the trail veering right.
25.6	Ride down the paved road 9 miles back to car/Big Pine.

The rolling hills of Coyote Flat and the Baker Creek plains. Cow Creek meanders in the foreground.

Continuation to Bishop Alternative:

11.0	From mile 11 on the above Mileage Guide, turn left at the split near Coyote Creek.
12.6	Cross creek and climb up the road. Soon awesome views

	of the Whites will loom in front of the descent ahead! (there will be a couple uphill sections first).
13.5	You'll pass by pillars of rock and groves of pinyon pines on rad bermed turns.
14.8	After this last small uphill section, the road will gradually steepen and become rockier.
20.4	Keep straight (left) on main road.
21.0	Stay left at the powerlines, staying on the main dirt road.
23.0	Here, you'll reach a paved road and the end of the ride. If you left your shuttle in Bishop, go left on Reata Rd.

Black Canyon Ride

Looking across the Owens Valley at the Sierras above Black Canyon.

Location: White Mountains east of Bishop.
Distance: 9.7 miles one way (more miles are possible).
Elevation: 8640/4100 ft.

Trail Surface: 18% singletrack; 82% narrow dirt/rocky road.
Type of Ride: One-Way Shuttle ride.
Terrain: High desert; rugged spires; limestone canyons; jagged peaks; Sierra and Owen's Valley views; pinion pine; juniper; sage; mine shafts.
Technical Level: Very Difficult; full suspension type of ride.
Exertion Level: Moderate.

Scenic wonders abound at every turn!

Highlights: Welcome to the mighty White Mountains; the most unknown of the "14-er" ranges in the country! (At 14,246 feet tall, White Mountain Peak is not much lower than the record-holder Mount Whitney). Even more impressive, however, is that these mountains tower 10,000 feet above neighboring Owen's Valley. The Whites are home to the most ancient living species in the world; the gnarled Ancient Bristlecone Pines. Predating many ancient civilizations, some of these Bristlecone Pines are almost 5,000 years old! Also thriving in this stark and solitary range, desert bighorn sheep can be spotted, along with golden eagles, falcons, the sage grouse and shrews. Notably, the ground these animals walk on consists of primeval sedimentary rocks, which are filled with 600 million year old fossils. The White Mountains also contain the largest adjoining area of alpine steppe above 10,000 ft. in the contiguous United States.

Black Canyon is a special gem in this land of extremes. With a 4500 foot drop on everything from smooth singletrack to a boulder-strewn jeep route, Black Canyon makes for an extremely epic ride! Its bound to impress any adventure-minded mountain biker with the world-class scenery and terrain!

Dropping into Black Canyon.

Options: Some locals bike a steeper version of the ride that starts at the top of Black Canyon near Schulman Grove at 10500 ft. Unfortunately, the entry and top section of this road is in the Ancient Bristlecone Pine Forest, which prohibits bikes.

Extremely hard core cardio-freak riders (no exaggeration here) may want to crank out a mega loop by riding up Silver Canyon Road out of Bishop and then along White Mountain Road to Black Canyon. This 36 mile loop climbs 6,300 feet before giving any relief.

Note: Be self-sufficient! Take extra tubes and patches! Wearing layers is a good idea since the top of the ride can be 20-30 degrees cooler than the lower section of the ride. Also, note that most of the White Mountains are open for biking, with the exception of the Ancient Bristlecone Forest.

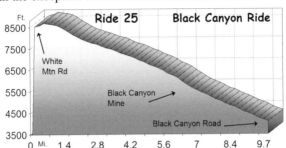

Directions/Access: This ride involves a fairly long shuttle. Leave one car at the end of the ride near Bishop. Drive a couple miles south of Bishop and turn left on Warm Springs Road. After about 4 ½ miles the road will turn into the graded dirt "Black Canyon Road." Stay on this road for approximately 2.5 miles as it turns south and follows the base of the mountains until a road split. The shuttle drop off is at this first major intersection: at a large right-hand curve in the road, Black Canyon Road will veer off to the left and head up into the mountains. Park on the side of the road here, as there is no official parking area.

To reach the trailhead, drive back to HWY 395 and head south to Big Pine. Go left on SR-168/Westguard Pass for 13 miles and then turn left on White Mountain Road. Parking is in the dirt pullout on the left-hand side of White Mountain Road (at a curve in the road) about 1.1 miles above the Grand View Campground.

Black Canyon Mine.

The rocky trail drops steeply through Black Canyon.

Mileage Guide

.00	From the trailhead/parking area off of White Mountain Road, take the dirt road leading north. (The road is somewhat faint and doubletrack-like at first). As you ride into pinion pine forest, you'll spot the Sierra Nevada to the west and desert mountains to the east. Just ahead, a fainter road heads down to the left; ignore this road!
.20	Split! Go left (straight) on the trail.
.60	As the trail starts to head downhill along the steep slope, don't miss the views of the valley!
1.5	The trail will turn more into an old road, although the bermed-out track within the road is hard to miss!
2.0	Split! Go left and downhill. [There are options here for those who enjoy exploring and would like to tack on some extra riding mileage. By going right, you can merge onto the top section of Black Canyon Road, which climbs to a spring and some old cabins. In .2 miles, go right at the road split. In another .2 miles, stay

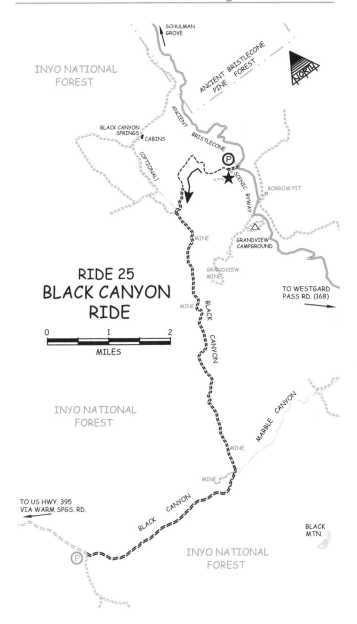

SCHULMAN GROVE

INYO NATIONAL FOREST

ANCIENT BRISTLECONE PINE FOREST

NORTH

BLACK CANYON SPRINGS

CABINS

ANCIENT BRISTLECONE

(OPTIONAL)

P

SCENIC BYWAY

BORROW PIT

MINE

GRANDVIEW CAMPGROUND

GRANDVIEW MINE

TO WESTGARD PASS RD. (168)

RIDE 25
BLACK CANYON
RIDE

MINE

BLACK CANYON

0   1   2
MILES

MINE

MARBLE CANYON

INYO NATIONAL FOREST

MINE

MINE

TO US HWY. 395
VIA WARM SPGS. RD.

BLACK CANYON

P

BLACK MTN.

INYO NATIONAL FOREST

	right as you ride around a corner and up a little hill. Soon you will be riding along a creek. You'll reach the cabins in another mile. The road continues beyond this point but soon becomes very steep and unridable as it ascends to White Mountain Road near Schulman Grove.]
2.1	Merge onto the main road. This will eventually lead into an orange-colored canyon area with progressively narrower, bermed, and rockier sections of road.
3.7	The ride passes a mine off to the right.
5.4	After passing a lush spring area, which may be overgrown, you will enter the Black Canyon.
6.3	As you are riding through a mega-rocky section, spot the large mineshaft on the left. This is Black Canyon Mine.
6.7	As you keep heading straight downhill, you'll pass some old mining roads and an offshoot to Marble Canyon. The landscape will become more barren as the road straightens into a high speed section.
9.7	Major intersection and end of the ride. Visible from this location are the Palisade Glacier to the southwest, Wheeler Crest to the northwest and Owens Valley and Bishop to the north.

The ride commences with excellent singletrack overlooking the Sierra Mountain Range to the west.

Other White Mountains Rides

A. White Mountain Peak

While most people have never even hiked a "14-er," White Mountain Peak (14,246 feet) offers a bikable option! This jeep road ride is an epic test of endurance. The payoff is some of the most incredible and unimpeded views of the entire Sierra Nevada Range and the expanse of California and Nevada. As it is the highest road in California, you can earn the bragging rights of having biked at such extreme altitude.

The 7-mile "south-face route" starts at Barcroft gate at the end of White Mountain Road. To get here from Mammoth Lakes or Bishop, take HWY 395 south to Big Pine. Go left on the SR-168/Westguard Pass for 13 miles and then turn left on White Mountain Road. Take this all the way (27 miles) to the end at Barcroft Gate at 12,000 feet. Note that the last 17 miles is on a somewhat rough dirt/gravel road.

B. Silver Canyon

From Bishop, a "ridable" dirt road winds its way up Silver Canyon up to White Mountain Road at 10,400 feet - making for a 6,300 vertical foot climb. Diehard bikers test their stamina on this ride. Typically, it's ridden as an out & back; about 12 miles each way (depending on where you start).

To reach Silver Canyon Road, drive HWY 395 south to Bishop and then go left on HWY 6. In about 4 miles, turn right on Silver Canyon Road. There are dirt pullouts in various places up the road, or you can park at Laws Museum.

Not to minimize the very difficult Silver Canyon ride, but the ultimate endurance test for those who want Eco-Challenge training is to ride up Silver Canyon Road to White Mountain

Peak. This provides over 10,000 feet of vertical terrain for those who can handle unimaginable suffering.

Another very difficult option is to ride up Silver Canyon to White Mountain Road and down to the Black Canyon Ride, making an extremely strenuous 36 mile loop.

C. Wyman Road

Wyman Road descends down the east side of the White Mountains and passes through creeks, boulders, old cabins, Roberts Ranch, petroglyphs, meadows, and Bristlecone Pines. Additionally, there are plenty of amazing eastward desert views of Deep Springs, Fish Valley, and mountains beyond. There are endless spur roads to explore, camp, and hike around. Ranging from White Mountain Road near the top of Silver Canyon down to SR-168, Wyman Road is about 21 miles one way.

To ride this as a one-way shuttle, take HWY 395 to 168/ Westguard Pass. Continue on about 29 miles to the bottom of Wyman Creek Road near the old Caltrans station. Drop a car here. To reach the top of Wyman Canyon Road, drive back to the turnoff for White Mountain Road and drive up to Schulman Grove. There is parking at the Schulman Grove visitor center.

Wyman Road shadowed in an approaching thunder storm.

An old cabin in the White Mountains.

D. Crooked & Cottonwood Creek Roads

Descending the east side of the White Mountains, both Crooked Creek Road and Cottonwood Creek Roads offer a unique landscape. However, both these roads eventually dead-end, unless you can find the various obscure animal and Native American trails that occasionally spur off. Cottonwood Creek actually contains a little ridable singletrack that follows part of the creek along some beautiful aspen trees. Both roads enter some of the most scenic areas in the White Mountains and pass several cabins.

Crooked Creek Road is located off of White Mountain Road. It is about 19.5 miles from the intersection of highway 168 and White Mountain Road, or about 9.5 miles past Schulman Grove where the road turns to dirt. Crooked Creek Road veers right and is marked with a sign. The first mile is well traveled by students and researchers, in fast travelling autos, from the White Mountain Research Station nearby. Cottonwood Creek Road is accessed about a mile down Crooked Creek Road, and is also signed.

North of Mammoth

Big Springs Loop

In the forest above Big Springs.

Location: North of Mammoth off of Owens River Road.

Distance: 4.1 miles. (Many more miles are possible).

Elevation: 7280/7750 ft.

Trail Surface: 16% mx singletrack; 44% narrow dirt roads; 40% graded dirt road.

Type of Ride: Loop.

Terrain: Jeffrey pine forest; Bald Mountain views; Owens River.

Technical Level: Medium; smooth loose dirt, some mx whoops.

Exertion Level: Moderate.

Highlights: Hidden deep in a peaceful Jeffrey pine forest, Big Springs is a fantastic area to ride around - especially if you are staying in the Big Springs Campground. Big Springs is the water source for much of the spring-fed upper Owens River.

This ride winds its way through the forest along ridges and knolls with sporadic mountain views. The initial climb is on a graded dirt road, and most of the downhill sections are on sandier narrow roads and trails. Because of high motorcycle use, many of the roads have "whoops," large bumps/jumps that can either make the ride more exciting and fun or annoying - depending on the rider. The ride is short enough to check it out either way.

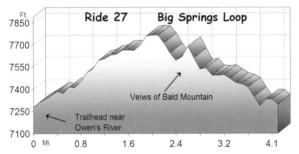

Options: Unlimited miles of road can lengthen and shorten your ride here. You may want to explore the road along Owens River or check out Big Springs at the end of Deadman Creek. Extension rides to Bald Mountain and Clark Canyon are described below in "Other Rides Nearby."

Note: This area is fairly popular with offroad motorcycles. Remember that they can't hear you coming!

Enjoying a solitary section of forested singletrack.

Directions/Access: Take HWY 395 north from Mammoth Lakes. After about 7 miles turn right on "Owens River Road" and continue for a couple miles. Turn left on the road that leads to Big Springs Campground (2S04). Passing the campground, stay right on road 2S04. After crossing over the creek, drive approximately 400 yards farther and park in the large dirt pullout on the right (just before the main road turns to dirt). You will see a sign that says "Vehicle Restriction Area."

Mileage Guide	
.00	From the parking area, ride up the main paved road. It will soon become a graded dirt road. Stay on this main road for the next mile.
1.1	Go left on the road labeled "I" and "2S03" and continue climbing up this road.
1.4	When the road splits, turn right.
1.7	Turn right on the dirt road. It will be flat before turning into a whooped-out downhill section.
2.2	Merge left on the road. Just ahead a singletrack merges left off of the road; take this.
2.3	Cross the road and continue riding up the trail. Depending on the conditions, this next (short-but-steep) section may be a sandy mess – gather up some speed and try to charge through! If it hasn't rained in awhile, anybody but superman will be walking up.
2.4	After reaching the top of this knoll, follow the whooped motorcycle trail down.
2.7	Views of Bald Mountain on the left! Keep pedaling by the road that heads down to the right.
2.9	Ignore another road heading to the right. Soon the road will narrow into more of a trail!
3.2	When you reach a main road, go right and then pass by the road on the left.
3.3	As the road heads downhill, look for the singletrack veering off to the left. Take it!
3.4	After a short uphill, you'll come into an open area with

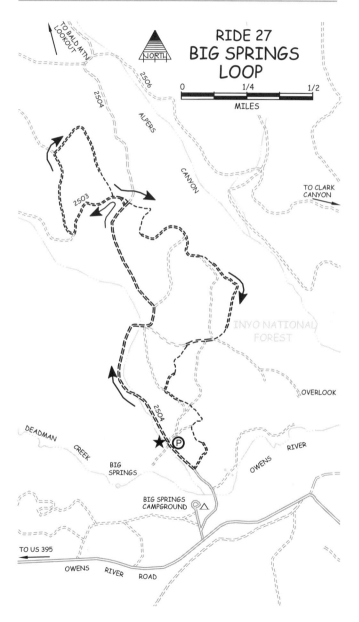

RIDE 27
BIG SPRINGS
LOOP

	mountain views to the west and Bald Mountain behind. Proceed downhill.
3.6	Stay high on the hill by veering left and avoiding the roads off to the right. The trail will soon become single-track once again.
3.7	At the 4-way intersection, continue riding straight ahead.
3.8	At the next split, stay left and crank up a short uphill.
4.0	Go right at the main road, 2S04, to finish the loop.
4.1	Loop complete.

Other Riding Nearby

Making turns on the Big Springs Loop with Bald Mountain behind.

A. Bald Mountain

While it's not a technically challenging ride, many riders like to add the 10 miles each-way by riding up Road 2S04 ("A") to Indian Summit and onto Road 1S05 ("D") to Bald Mountain. The breathtaking views at the lookout station at the top make it well worth it. Among the many sights, you will spot the White Mountains, Crowley lake, a huge span of the Sierra

Range, Glass Flow Ridge, Mono Craters and Mono Lake. An outhouse and a cabin are also on top. Alternative roads may be ridden back down; please consult a topo map if you are unfamiliar with the area. Note that bikes are not allowed off road in the Indian Summit Research Area. Riders can start at the Big Springs Campground, or at the dirt pullout described above under the Big Springs Loop Directions/Access.

B. Clark Canyon

A multi-sport extension of the Big Springs Loop is to ride into Clark Canyon, an excellent rock climbing area at the base of Bald Mountain. Mount Morrison and the surrounding Sierras add to the beauty. The ride, which is well traveled by rock climbers, is almost 6 miles each-way and passes through part of Alpers Canyon, past a meadow and up a ridge to Clark Canyon. Start at the parking area for the Big Springs Loop and ride up road 2S04. After about 2 miles, turn right on road 2S06. A sign that marks this road to Alpers and Clark Canyon has recently been missing, but hopefully has been replaced. You'll pass some roads veering off to both sides and then pass a cattle gate. About a half mile past the cattle gate, the road will merge with road 1S47 which comes in from the left. After passing another cattle gate and veering left on the road, you will pass through a meadow and around a ridge as you come into Clark Canyon. When you reach a 4-way intersection, turn right and ride toward the parking area. Trails ascend to the sport climbing spots from here.

C. Hartley Springs Loop

The so-called "Hartley Springs Mountain Bike Trail" is a 9.2 mile all-dirt road loop, with nearly 1,000 feet of climbing. While this ride is on somewhat boring forested dirt roads, it provides some good climbing and refreshing descents. Most of the uphill is finished after the first 3.4 miles, then it's a very long and gradual descent for the rest of the ride. The toughest part is climbing/descending one section of steep pumice road

The Trailhead.

toward the end of the ride. However, it's the views that make this ride worthwhile. Mono Lake and Mono Craters will be on display in a couple locations. A large viewpoint/pullout on the right is a great place to stop and contemplate the many wonders of creation, or just eat lunch. To the north, Aeolian Buttes guard Mono Lake and Pumice Valley. The views slightly over to the east reveal the Mono Craters; the newest mountain range in America. The northmost Panum Crater erupted only 600 years ago. The closest, most south, crater is Devils Punchbowl. Even farther east is Bald Mountain. The southwest is marked by Carson Peak; looking west (straight ahead) is Reversed Peak.

From Mammoth Lakes, take HWY 395 north about 14 miles. Before reaching June Lake, turn left on a dirt road directly across from Pumice Mine Road. Park in the pullout on the left, in front of the "Hartley Springs Mountain Bike Trail" sign.

Views of Mono Lake and the Mono Craters.

Obsidian Dome Bike Loop

The stumps constrict the old roads to prevent use from autos and ATVs.

Location: Between Mammoth Lakes and June Lake.

Distance: 4.8 miles.

Elevation: 8020/8430 ft.

Trail Surface: 45% trails and dirt roads that are being converted to singletrack; 55% graded dirt roads.

Type of Ride: Loop.

Terrain: Obsidian Dome; pine & fir forest; pumice meadows; campground; Red Tail Hawks and other wildlife.

Technical Level: Easy/Medium.

Exertion Level: Moderate.

Highlights: The Inyo National Forest has recently closed down many of the roads in the Hartley Springs Campground and Obsidian Dome areas under a new and much needed forest management plan. Some of the roads are now only open to non-motorized or 2-wheeled vehicles, and will hopefully soon become singletrack. These "trails" are marked by the large tree stumps used to constrict the entrances and exits of certain sections to bike-sized users. A small loop has been created, which is described in this ride. As these roads transform to singletrack, they will make a fun ride with a fairly easy climb and a nice weaving downhill section.

The ride skirts part of the Obsidian Dome, a 100-300 foot tall mountain of black volcanic glass. This mile-wide dome formed about 600 years ago when local eruptions released molten glass that quickly cooled and crystallized. The obsidian was prized by Native Americans for arrowheads and tools. To check out the different layers of obsidian and see views of the area, hike the dome.

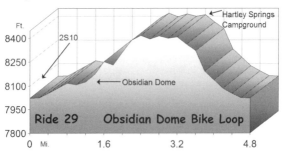

Options: There are many new OHV-designated routes in the area, that have some sandy singletrack. Depending on the conditions, these may be fun additions to the ride.

Note: The more bikers that ride, the quicker the singletrack will form!

Directions/Access: From Mammoth Lakes, take HWY 395 north 11 miles and turn left onto Obsidian Dome Road opposite from Bald Mountain Lookout. Park at the pullout by the Inyo National Forest sign.

Mileage Guide	
0.0	At the pullout, start riding straight up the road.
.70	Turn left at the trail marked by the stumps for a run through the pines.
1.0	Barge through a sandy switchback!
1.3	You'll pass through more of the stumps into an open area

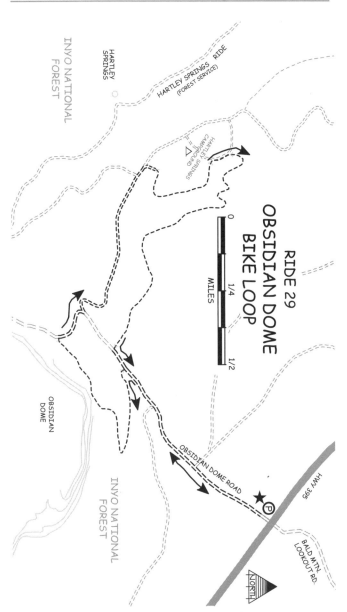

RIDE 29
OBSIDIAN DOME
BIKE LOOP

INYO FOREST

HARTLEY SPRINGS

HARTLEY SPRINGS RIDE
(FOREST SERVICE)

HARTLEY SPRINGS CAMPGROUND

INYO NATIONAL FOREST

OBSIDIAN DOME

INYO NATIONAL FOREST

OBSIDIAN DOME ROAD

HWY 395

BALD MTN LOOKOUT RD.

NORTH

MILES

0   1/4   1/2

	by Obsidian Dome, with sandy walking trails veering off. Stay left and climb up the rocky double track.
1.5	Pedal right on the main graded dirt road.
1.7	Make a sharp left up the road (it's paved at first).
2.4	Turn right into Hartley Springs Campground and veer right around the bathrooms. Soon you will see more stumps on the right; pass through and continue riding on a nice section of trail.
2.8	Another stump exit; ride right on the road. (Stay right ignoring the other camp roads).
2.9	Soon, you will pedal left through another set of stumps onto a trail that winds through packed pumice before dropping into the forest.
4.0	Exit the stumps and turn left on the main road to return to the start of the ride.
4.8	That's all biker-folks.

The Yost Meadow Trail cuts through groves of aspens.

Yost Meadow Trail

A biker's-eye view of Gull Lake.

Location: Off HWY 158 in June Lake.

Distance: 8 miles.

Elevation: 7700/9100 ft.

Trail Surface: 99% singletrack; 1% dirt road.

Type of Ride: Out & Back.

Terrain: Steep mountainside; sierra meadow; pine forest; aspen groves; creeks; chaparral; eagles; deer.

Technical Level: Difficult; some steep sections.

Exertion Level: Very Strenuous.

Highlights: A relatively unknown singletrack, this prized trail weaves its way above June Lake to Yost Meadow. The overly picturesque trail climbs a chaparral mountainside, passes through the June Mountain ski area, and then glides its way through groves of aspen trees and forest-bounded alpine meadows. The initial mile is the steepest, so be prepared to dis-

Its all singletrack on the Yost Meadow Trail.

mount a couple times. The benefits are reaped after the trail eases near Yost Meadow, which used to be a lake. You'll be left feeling like you just went backpacking and saw wonders that are not usually seen on a bike! Almost all downhill, the return trip is fun, fun, fun!

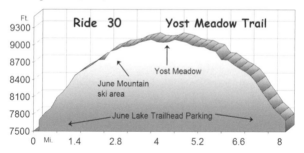

Options: Loops are possible with ski trails and roads on June Mountain. Some bikers opt to ride up to the top of June Mountain to glance over the Deadman Creek basin on one side and June and Mono Lake to the other (see mile 5.7 on the Mileage Guide).

Note: It is important to stay on the Yost Meadow Trail. Other trails, such as the Glass Creek Trail (which has almost disap-

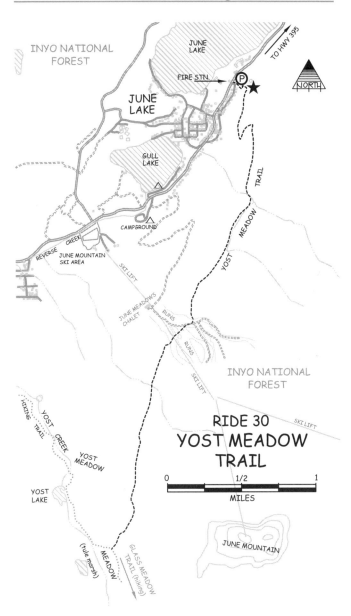

INYO NATIONAL FOREST

JUNE LAKE

TO HWY 395

FIRE STN.

NORTH

JUNE LAKE

GULL LAKE

CAMPGROUND

REVERSE CREEK

JUNE MOUNTAIN SKI AREA

SKI LIFT

JUNE MEADOWS CHALET

RUNS

RUNS

SKI LIFT

YOST MEADOW TRAIL

INYO NATIONAL FOREST

SKI LIFT

RIDE 30
YOST MEADOW TRAIL

0   1/2   1
MILES

HIKING TRAIL

YOST CREEK

YOST MEADOW

YOST LAKE

(tule marsh)

MEADOW

GLASS MEADOW TRAIL (hiking)

JUNE MOUNTAIN

A beautiful swampy remnant of a lake near Yost Meadow.

peared due to non-use), are recently off limits to bikes for unknown reasons.

Directions/Access: From Mammoth Lakes, take HWY 395 north about 20 miles to the south junction of June Lake Loop (158).   Just as you are driving into the town of June Lake (a little more than 2 miles from HWY 395), go left on the dirt road across from the large balancing boulder and the fire station. Park in the dirt pullout on the left. Just beyond, you'll see the sign marking the Trailhead.

Mileage Guide	
0.0	From the pullout parking area, ride up the dirt road to the left and pass the cabins on the right. Not far behind the wood sign labeled "Yost Meadow," there will be a large kiosk trail sign. Continue on the wide-at-first trail.
.10	Stay right on the steep singletrack.
.20	Attesting to the steepness of the trail, there are already incredible mountain-framed views of June and Gull Lakes.
.70	The terrain will gradually change from open sage brush mountainside to more ridable forest terrain.
2.2	Here, you emerge from the forest on to one of the June Mountain Ski runs. The trail is fainter through this next section. Take note of this area so you can find the trail on the way back. Usually a rock cairn or stacked logs

	mark the trail on the border of the ski run. As you come out onto the ski run, veer right and ride over a little gully. From here, ride out to the main road that heads down to the ski lifts. Immediately start looking for a fainter road/trail that heads off to the left. This will take you toward a dark gray metal shack.
2.3	In front of the gray shack, a wood sign labeled "Yost Meadow Trail" marks the route. Keep riding past this sign, and veer left (almost straight ahead) on a faint-at-first rocky singletrack heading west across the ski run.
2.8	Cross a small creek and continue on.
3.2	As you ride into another meadow area, enjoy the beautiful views.
4.0	After a quick downhill section, you'll arrive at a meadow and tule marsh. This a great place to hike around, look for wildlife, and enjoy serenity. Note that other trails split off here as well, but these are closed to biking. As this is an out & back ride, return via the same trails.
5.5	Pedal through the ski run area once again.
5.7	After passing by the gray metal shack, veer right up the hill a little, and then left over the gully (just before the dirt roads split 3-ways) and back onto the singletrack winding through the trees. [Another option to tack on some more uphill miles is to continue on up the dirt road to the top of June Mountain Ski Area]. Or, just head back the way you came; the trail resumes and bombs back through the forest and aspen groves.
6.9	The first crystal blue lake glimpses enhance the exhilarating descent!
8.0	All done.

Bennettville Trail

Descending singletrack toward Mine Creek.

Location: 40 miles north of Mammoth, off Tioga Pass.

Distance: 3 miles.

Elevation: 9725/9865 ft.

Trail Surface: Mostly singletrack following an old wagon road.

Type of Ride: Out & Back.

Terrain: Ghost town ruins; high alpine lakes; reflective ponds; lush valleys; sparse pine forest; creek; springs; wildflowers; granite outcroppings; mountain peak views.

Technical Level: Medium; easy with some rough rocky parts.

Exertion Level: Mild/Moderate.

Highlights: Both the high altitude singletrack treasure and the old remains of the scenic Bennettville ghost town, create a superb riding experience. Much of the ride follows the route of the Great Sierra Wagon Road. In the 1860's silver was dis-

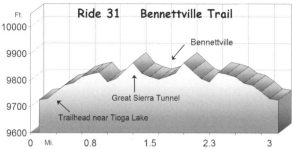

covered in the area, and by 1881 the Great Sierra Consolidated Silver Company purchased the existing claims and founded the town. Named after the president of the company, Bennettville featured the Great Sierra Tunnel which reached 1784 feet into the earth in attempt to connect different silver lodes. An ambitious 56 mile road, the Great Sierra Wagon Road, was also built to connect the town with a rail station in Yosemite. Segments of Tioga Pass Road follow this original wagon trail. With hundred's of thousands of dollars invested, bust came all too soon in 1884 as financial disaster hit and investors became skeptical at the lack of expected amounts of silver. Later the mine was briefly reopened and the tunnel lengthened to 2000 feet. When the mine failed to reach the silver ledge, Bennettville promptly became a fabled ghost town in 1889. Today, some of the original mining equipment is displayed in front of the tunnel. The assay office and a barn still stand overlooking Mine Creek. Sections of the Great Sierra wagon road may be seen, along with old trails, and other evidence of past settlement.

Water and rail tracks exit out of
The Great Sierra Tunnel.

Options: Riders may stash their bikes and continue hiking up Mine Creek to Shell Lake, Fantail Lake, and Spuller Lake. For additional biking miles, ride Saddlebag Lake Loop (Ride 32) just a few miles away.

The two original buildings still standing include a large barn and a restored office building.

Note: Hikers, equestrians and guided tours may be found on the trails. Be courteous and help keep singletrack open to bikes! Entering the mineshaft is not advised; the air is unsafe.

Directions/Access: From Mammoth lakes, drive north on HWY 395 about 25 miles. Turn left on 120/Tioga Pass near the Mobile Station by Mono Lake. Drive up toward Yosemite for approximately 11 miles, and then make a sharp right at the dirt road/small open parking area across from Tioga Lake. Park here. (This is roughly .4 miles past the Tioga Lake Campground). The old roadbed is blockaded by boulders, and just beyond a Forest Service sign depicts a biker symbol.   If you are driving from Yosemite, the trailhead is just under a mile beyond the park boundary.

Mileage Guide
0.0	The ride begins at the boulders blocking off the old road. What begins as a smooth road, will soon narrow down and often change from a rocky surface, to moist dirt, to grassy, and back to rocky. As you ride, you'll pass reflective ponds mirroring the unbeatable views of mountains, lakes, and valleys.

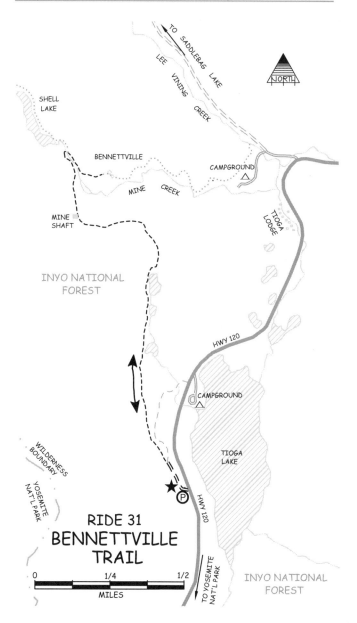

TO SADDLEBAG LAKE

LEE VINING CREEK

NORTH

SHELL LAKE

BENNETTVILLE

CAMPGROUND

MINE CREEK

TIOGA LODGE

MINE SHAFT

INYO NATIONAL FOREST

HWY 120

CAMPGROUND

TIOGA LAKE

WILDERNESS BOUNDARY

YOSEMITE NAT'L PARK

HWY 120

P

RIDE 31
BENNETTVILLE
TRAIL

0   1/4   1/2

MILES

TO YOSEMITE NAT'L PARK

INYO NATIONAL FOREST

1.0	Just before the trail surface turns to broken shale, you may be able to spot the old Bennettville barn far off to your right through the trees.
1.2	Check out the Great Sierra Tunnel mineshaft! A small creek and railroad tracks run out of the tunnel where authentic mining machinery is scattered around. The trail continues past the tunnel and heads down toward Mine Creek and Bennettville.
1.3	Just ahead the trail splits. Go right and use the logs to cross over the creek. (The trail to the left heads upstream to Shell Lake). After crossing the creek, a few trails criss-cross and split off. Most of these head to Bennettville just a short jaunt ahead.
1.5	You first notice the old barn and office buildings as you come to the historic Bennettville. You may want to get off the bike and explore around for more evidence of the 19th century settlement. Hiking up Mine Creek will lead to some pristine Sierra lakes. To complete the ride, pedal back the way you came.
3.0	Trailhead.

Bennettville Trail just above Tioga Lake.

Saddlebag Lake Trail

Enjoying the serenity of a late season Saddlebag Lake ride.

Location: 38 miles north of Mammoth, off Tioga Pass.

Distance: 4.2 miles.

Elevation: 10,060/10160 ft.

Trail Surface: 96% singletrack; 4% dirt road.

Type of Ride: Loop.

Terrain: Majestic high alpine lake; austere open spaces; pine forest; meadows; glaciers; creeks; mountain peaks.

Technical Level: Medium/Difficult; some more difficult shale and large rocks in the trail, especially on the last section.

Exertion Level: Mild; although the elevation is very high.

Highlights: Nestled between Hoover Wilderness and Yosemite National Park, Saddlebag Lake loop is a scenic mountain bike blessing! This gorgeous high-altitude riding is almost all singletrack varying from smooth dirt to shale and more difficult rocky sections. While the elevation doesn't vary much, there are plenty of short changes in elevation to keep it interesting. Mount Conness and glaciers tower over much of the ride, as do White Mountain, Tioga Peak and the Dore Cliffs.

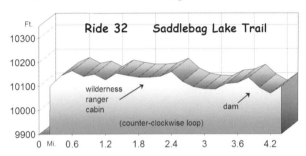

Options: Since the ride is relatively short, combining it with the Bennettville Trail (Ride 31) makes for a great day of biking! Ride 33 is also nearby. You may want to stash the bikes and hike or fish; this is an amazing area to chill out and relax!

Note: Do not bike on any other trails or into Wilderness areas!!! Keep this trail legal for bikes by staying on the Saddlebag Lake Trail only! Also be courteous of fisherman and hikers; this is a popular area.

Riding near the edge of Yosemite.

Directions/Access: From Mammoth lakes, drive north on HWY 395 about 25 miles. Turn left on 120/Tioga Pass near the Mobile Station by Mono Lake. Take this for almost 10 miles before turning right at the "Saddlebag Lake" sign. Drive up this slow and bumpy road for about 2 ½ miles and park beyond the campground roads near the restrooms.

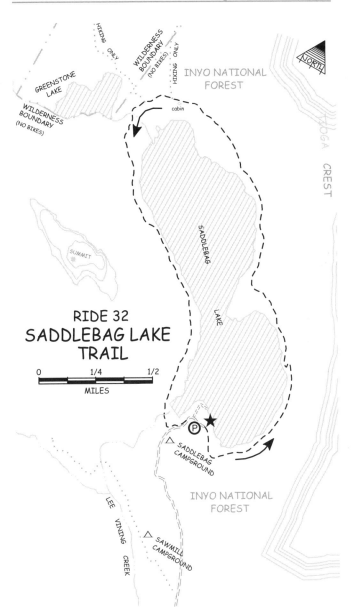

HIKING ONLY

GREENSTONE LAKE

WILDERNESS BOUNDARY (NO BIKES)

WILDERNESS BOUNDARY (NO BIKES)

HIKING ONLY

INYO NATIONAL FOREST

NORTH

TIOGA CREST

cabin

SADDLEBAG LAKE

SUMMIT

RIDE 32
SADDLEBAG LAKE
TRAIL

0   1/4   1/2
MILES

P

SADDLEBAG CAMPGROUND

INYO NATIONAL FOREST

LEE VINING CREEK

SAWMILL CAMPGROUND

Mileage Guide	
0.0	Ride north, past the restrooms, to the trailhead sign and gate at the end of the lot. Follow the old graded road, that soon narrows down to singletrack.
2.2	The cabin on the left houses the wilderness ranger.
2.4	Ignore the trail to the right, which leads into the designated Wilderness. Keep to the left as you continue riding around the lake.
2.5	Pass over the creek on logs and continue on the trail as it soon leads into a meadow area.
3.3	Most will test their biking skills as they negotiate through some gnarly shale and rocks.
3.8	After passing the dam, cruise down the trail on the left, over the creek, past the gate, and up to the main road.
4.0	Near the green building, turn left on the road and ride back to the parking area.
4.2	Loop complete!

Lake Canyon Trail

Location: North of Mammoth, near Lundy Lakes.
Distance: 6.4 miles.
Elevation: 7820/9700 ft.
Trail Surface: 25% singletrack; 75% doubletrack.
Type of Ride: Out & Back.
Terrain: Steep canyon; small lakes; creek; waterfall; high altitude mountains; views; shale; mines.
Technical Level: Medium/Difficult; a rough trail.
Exertion Level: Very Strenuous; very steep climbing.

Highlights: The historic Lake Canyon Trail climbs the serendipitous canyon to Lake Oneida and the 1880's gold mine, May Lundy Mine. This gorgeous canyon, with walls

A rapidly approaching thunderstorm darkens the northern skies.

made up of Gilcrest Peak to the east and Mount Scowden on the west, is a hanging glacial valley above Lundy Canyon. If you love steep climbs with remote backcountry scenery, this is your ride! Lake Canyon Trail, mostly a rough doubletrack, climbs almost 2,000 feet in just over 3 miles to the mining ruins. On its way up, it crosses an aspen-lined creek a few times making it a spectacular Fall colors ride. This trail/road is special since it is one of the only trails adjacent to Wilderness that still allows bicycle riding, while banning all motor vehicles. It is primarily used by hikers and backpackers exploring the lakes and mines.

You'll want to save time for hiking around the May Lundy Mine, which has an amazing amount of remains leftover from the 1880's. Along with rail tracks leading out of a mine shaft, there are extensive mill

A mineshaft near Lake Oneida.

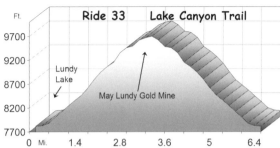

remnants, a cable tram system, tattered cabins, and plenty of other mining equipment scattered about. There is an abundance of mines to explore, but the actual May Lundy mine shaft is situated high up the mountainside above, extending over 1500 feet into the mountain.

Options: Stash the bikes and keep hiking!

Note: This trail leads right up to the Wilderness boundary, in which bikes are strictly prohibited. Even though the road keeps going, the boundary is near the tailings of the mineshaft near the mill ruins. To explore the lake and mine artifacts, you should leave your bike at the boundary and continue on foot.

Directions/Access: From Mammoth Lakes, take HWY 395 32 miles north (7 miles past Lee Vining). Turn left at the road signed Lundy Lake; opposite 167 East. After driving up 3.5 miles, turn left on Lundy Dam Road and park at the dam.

Mileage Guide	
0.0	Ride past the locked gate and start climbing above the lake.
2.1	Cross Lake Canyon Creek!
3.0	To the left, you'll pass Blue and Crystal "Lakes."
3.2	When you come upon the tailings from a mineshaft above right, the wilderness boundary now crosses the road. There are no bikes allowed past this point. To continue on to the Oneida Lake and May Lundy Mine, stash your bike and hike the remainder of the way. After exploring, return the same way. Enjoy all that downhill!
6.4	End of the line.

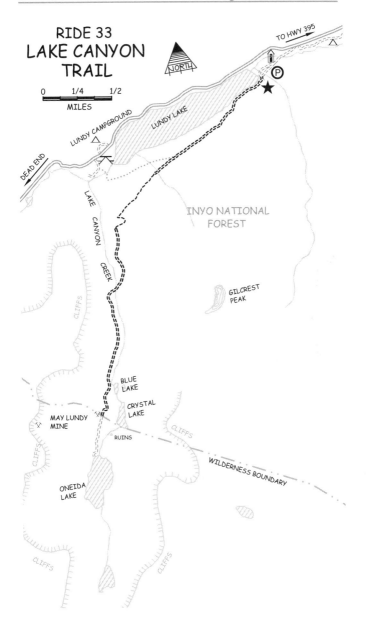

Hotsprings

Hot Creek

This is the mother of hot springs in the area and the crowds prove it. As Hot Creek flows toward the Owens River, it passes though a gorgeous canyon of ancient lakebed deposits interlaid with volcanic ash and tuff. The Yellowstone-like features of bubbling pools, steam vents, and other strange volcanic phenomena attract many gawkers. In two particular spots in the middle of the creek, hot steam vents up from the magma depths warming the water. Because it's in the creek, these hot springs occasionally have cooler currents mixing in with the hot flows. Bikers and other outdoor-sports enthusiasts love to come soak in the mineral-rich water after a long high altitude workout. Restrooms, changing rooms and paved parking are located up above the creek. Hot Creek is open from sunrise to sunset and bathing suits are required. To reach Hot Creek, drive south on 395 about 3 miles from the Mammoth/HWY 203 Junction. Turn left at the signed turnoff: "Hot Creek Hatchery/Airport." Make the first signed right and continue a couple miles on gravel road.

Keough Hot Springs

Located seven miles south of Bishop off HWY 395, Keough Hot Springs claims the "largest natural hot springs pool in the Eastern Sierra" with a mega 128-degree flow of 10 gallons every second from the source. This historic spa/resort has recently been renovated and includes a snack bar, picnic area, rock gardens, gift and swim shop, and camping/lodging facilities. Of course, the soothing hot mineral water is the main attraction. Call 760-872-4670 for more information.

Whitmore Pool

Whitmore Pool is a very scenic public pool fed by hot springs. Operated by Parks and Recreation Department, use of the facility requires a small fee. Surrounded by panoramic views of the Sierra and White Mountains, the facility has a 6-lane 25-meter pool, children's wading pool, restrooms, hot showers, and a BBQ/lawn area. Baseball fields are also in the area. The pool is open all summer and employs certified lifeguards. Call 760-934-8989 ext. 222 for updated info on fees, free swim days, and lap swim times. Whitmore Pool is located about 5 ½ miles south of the Mammoth Lakes exit on HWY 395. Turn east on Benton Crossing Road and drive or bike for one mile. The pool is on the right.

The Old House at Benton Hot Springs

Enjoy one of six redwood tubs in a lush setting while gasping at the great White Mountains. Benton Hot Springs is a quiet and relaxing enclave back-dropped against the dramatic Montgomery Peak and Boundary Peak. A natural hot spring of 135 degrees mixes with cold water to make a comfortable temperature. The tubs are on the Old House property, which dates to the 1860's silver mining boom. Antiques, arts and crafts, and artifacts fill the area. There is camping and a bed & breakfast nearby. To visit Benton Hot Springs, drive south on HWY 395 about 5 ½ miles to Benton Crossing Road. Take this 36 miles and merge onto HWY 120 East for about 3 miles. From Bishop, take HWY 6 about 36 miles and turn left onto HWY 120 for 4 miles. If you are driving from June Lake/Lee Vining area, take HWY 120 East 46 miles.

Good whole-some fun in the mountains.

Local Camping

The following list contains Inyo National Forest campgrounds near Mammoth, unless otherwise noted. To make a reservation call, 1.877.444.6777 or 760.9249.5500. For a complete list of campgrounds in the Eastern Sierra, see:
http://www.fs.fed.us/r5/inyo/recreation/campgrounds.html
The information below is subject to change depending on weather/conditions, deer migration, or policy changes.

Mammoth Lakes General Area					
Campground	*Fee*	*Dates*	*Max Stay*	*Sites*	*Elevation*
New Shady Rest	$12	5/11-10/28	14 days	94	7,800 ft.
Old Shady Rest	$12	6/8-9/16	14 days	51	7,800 ft.
Sherwin Creek	$12	5/4-9/16	21 days	87	7,600 ft.
Pine Glen	$12	as needed	14 days	11	7,800 ft.
Mammoth Lakes Basin					
Campground	*Fee*	*Dates*	*Max Stay*	*Sites*	*Elevation*
Coldwater	$13	6/8-9/16	14 days	77	8,900 ft.
Twin Lakes	$13	5/25-10/31	7 days	95	8,700 ft.
Lake George	$13	6/8-9/16	7 days	16	9,000 ft.
Lake Mary	$13	6/1-9/16	14 days	48	8,900 ft.
Pine City	$13	6/1-9/16	14 days	10	8,900 ft.
Red's Meadow Area					
Campground	*Fee*	*Dates*	*Max Stay*	*Sites*	*Elevation*
Agnew Meadows	$12	6/15-9/19	14 days	21	8,400 ft.
Minaret Falls	$12	6/15-9/19	14 days	27	7,600 ft.
Reds Meadow	$12	6/15-10/12	14 days	56	7,600 ft.
Pumice Flat	$12	6/15-9/19	14 days	17	7,700 ft.
Soda Springs	$12	6/15-9/8	14 days	29	7,700 ft.

Non-Forest Service Campgrounds				
Campground	*Phone*	*Fee*	*Sites*	*Elevation*
Devil's Postpile	1.800.365.camp	$16	21	7,600 ft
Mammoth Mtn RV Park	760.934.3822	$21+	227	7,800 ft.
Camp High Sierra	760.934.2368	$22+	N/A	8,200 ft.

Local Bike Shops

Footloose Sports   760.934.2400
3043 Main Street, Mammoth Lakes

Mammoth Sporting Goods   760.934.3239
1 Sierra Center Mall (Old Mammoth Road), Mammoth Lakes

Adventure Center   760.934.2571
Adventure Center at Mammoth Mountain, Mammoth Lakes

Brian's Bicycles & Cross Country Skis   760.924.8566
3059 Chateau Road (off Old Mammoth Rd), Mammoth Lakes

High Sierra Cycle Center   760.924.3723
(Custom frame fitting & cycling biomechanics)
123 Commerce Drive, Mammoth Lakes

Bikes of Bishop   760.872.3829
651 North Main Street, Bishop

Value Sports Bishop   760.873.3472
1331 Rocking W Dr (off HWY 395), Bishop

Local Bike Events

NORBA U.S. Mountain Bike National Championships
The godzilla of all races has returned to Mammoth Mountain!
Check out the big shots racing cross-country, short-track,
downhill, mountain cross, dual slalom, super D, and observed
trials during the last weekend of September.

Village Championships
Mammoth Sporting Goods has historically sponsored free
cross country and downhill races during the summer. Check
out the store on Old Mammoth Road for details and times.

Weekly Rides
Group rides in the area have been organized by Mammoth
Sporting Goods twice a week in the summer. Go by the store
on Old Mammoth Road for details and times. Weekly rides
have also been conducted by Footloose Sports, located at the
intersection of Main Street and Old Mammoth Road.

Local Resources

Mammoth Ranger Station and Visitor Center
760.924.5500/www.fs.fed.us/r5/inyo
PO Box 148 Mammoth CA, 93546-0148

Inyo National Forest Supervisor's Office
760.873.2400/873 N. Main Street, Bishop, CA 93514

Mono Basin Scenic Area Visitor Center &Ranger Station
760.647.3045 (Visitor Center)/760.647.3000 (Ranger Station)
PO Box 429, Lee Vining, CA 93541-0429

White Mountain Ranger Station
760.873.2500 (Ranger Station)/760.873.2573 (Visitor Center)
798 N. Main Street, Bishop, CA 93514

MAMBO (Mammoth Area Mountain Bike Organization)
760.934.1674/PO Box 93546, Mammoth Lakes, CA 93546

Mammoth Local Weather
760.934.7669/www.mammothweather.com

Visitors Bureau
888.GO.MAMMOTH/888.466.2666/www.visitmammoth.com

Town of Mammoth Lakes
760.934.8989/www.ci.mammoth-lakes.ca.us

The C.R.E.S.T. (Carson Ridgecrest Eastern Sierra Transit)
760.872.1901/www.countyofinyo.org/transit/CRESTpage.htm

Y.A.R.T.S. (Yosemite Area Rapid Transit)
1.888.98.YARTS/1.877.989.2728/www.yarts.com

Inyo Mono Transit (Various Routes; bicycles are permitted)
800.922.1930/www.countyofinyo.org/transit/transit.htm

The skyline on Ride15.

Index of Top 3 Trails by Category

Priceless Sierra gold:
Autumn - Yost Meadows

Index of Trails & Rides

Photos are located on page numbers in bold, while maps are in italicized pages below.

Riding along Lower Rock Creek; Ride 22.

The Authors

Dave and Allison love mountain biking in the Mammoth Lakes area, taking photographs, making maps, and hanging outside in nature! They wrote this book to share the passion!

Book Information

Additional copies of *Mountain Biking Mammoth* can be ordered at www.extremeline.com. For more information on purchasing books, email orders@extremeline.com.

If you have any questions, suggestions, or comments about the book or Extremeline Productions LLC, please email them to info@extremeline.com.

Extremeline Mountain Bike Guides also available:
Mountain Biking Santa Cruz
ISBN 0-9723361-0-9

WWW.EXTREMELINE.COM

What more can be said?